BIBLE
ANIMAL

TALES

50 DEVOTIONALS
FOR TWEEN-AGERS

BIBLE
ANIMAL
TALES

MARY ROSE PEARSON
ILLUSTRATED BY KERRY ADCOCK

Cover design by Cristina Fernández-Mershon
Manuscript format by Cristina Fernández-Mershon

ISBN 0-9664803-7-6

Library of Congress Control Number 2004112741

Printed in the United States of America

Fair Havens Publications®
P. O. Box 1238
Gainesville, TX 76241-1238
Web Site: www.fairhavenspub.com

*To the many wonderful
children who attended
my kids' crusades and
vacation Bible schools
through the years, to
the thousands who
professed Jesus as
Savior, and to those
who will read this book.*

*May God bless each of
you! Keep on keeping
on for Jesus till He
comes again!*

CONTENTS

INTRODUCTION

This is a devotion book for tweenagers (ages 8-12 or so) to read and enjoy for themselves. Or it can be used by parents in home devotions or by teachers in various church situations, in Bible clubs, or in home or Christian schools. Each devotion includes facts about animals, Bible stories that include animals, a personal application, and a learning activity. (Note to teachers: the publisher gives permission for you to photocopy the learning activity for use in classrooms.)

Every Bible story in *Bible Animal Tales* has at least one animal in it. The word animal, as it is used in this book, refers to the animal kingdom and includes all living creatures except people — insects, birds, creatures that live in the water, reptiles, and land animals. It is interesting to see how many animals are involved in some way in Bible stories. The focus of the Bible stories, though, is on the people and their relationship to God, not on the animals.

The Bible stories are in chronological order, which will help children to get a sense of Bible history as they proceed. The section "Animal Facts" gives some general information about animals, but it especially tells about the animals in relation to the people and events of Bible times. The section "How This Animal Tale Can Help You" shows children how to apply the Bible truths to their own lives.

It is my prayer that our Lord will use this book to be a blessing to many children, to help them know the Bible better, to encourage them to live godly lives, and to trust Christ as Savior if they have not yet done so.

MARY ROSE PEARSON

1
THE ORIGIN OF ALL ANIMALS

"Every animal of the forest is mine, and the cattle on a thousand hills. I know every bird in the mountains, and the creatures of the field are mine."
—Psalm 50:10, 11

Where did animals come from? The theory of evolution claims this:

1. All living things came from non-living elements (not by God's special creation).

2. First, there was a single cell. From it, more complex creatures developed over millions of years. One kind of creature gradually developed into another kind. At last, there were tiny animals, then bigger ones.

3. Man was the last creature to develop, and he came from the same ape-like creature that produced the monkey and the gorilla.

What's more, says this theory, all this happened by chance!

A theory is a belief—not proven facts. The Bible is more than just a theory; it is a revelation from God. God tells us in the Bible how He created all the animals and the rest of the universe. More proven facts support creation by God than the theory of evolution. Look at the facts:

ANIMAL FACTS
⊢ALL ANIMALS⊣

Who was present when animals came into existence? God was. He has always lived. He tells in the Bible how animals came into being.

How did animals begin? God created all animal life (mammals, birds, fish, amphibians, reptiles, and insects). He made each one after its own kind. One animal did not develop from another kind.

When did animals begin? God made animals on the fifth and sixth days of creation. Each day of creation was a 24-hour day.

What were the first animals like? They were perfect and fully developed.

When did people come into existence? God made two people on the sixth day after He created the animals. He gave every human being a spirit that lives forever and can know God and fellowship with Him.

How are people different from animals? Since people are made in the image of God and animals are not, they can't communicate with God in the same way people do.

BIBLE ANIMAL TALE
HOW ANIMALS BEGAN
(GENESIS 1:1–31; 2:19–20)

In the beginning, there were no animals. There was no universe—just a black, vast emptiness. But God and heaven existed. God never had a beginning. He has always lived.

All animals had their beginning in two days. "In the beginning God created the heavens and the earth." God created the earth to be a home for people and other living creatures. In the first four days, God made the earth ready for them.

God created light and separated it from the darkness. He made the sky. He brought the waters together, and the dry ground appeared. He made plants and trees to grow on the ground. He caused the sun, moon, and stars to shine.

On the fifth day, God created every living and moving thing in the waters. Freshwater fish filled the lakes and streams. All kinds of salt-water fish swam in the seas. God made turtles and other creatures that could swim in the waters and crawl on the land. Also on the fifth day, God made birds, from the tiny hummingbird to the huge ostrich.

On the sixth day God made all the land animals, each according to its kind. He made the little flea, the huge elephant, and all sizes in between. Each kind of animal was different from any other kind. For example, the giraffe has a long neck; the porcupine has quills; and the kangaroo has a pouch to hold its babies.

Also on the sixth day, God made a man and a woman, Adam and Eve, in His own image. God told Adam, "Rule over the fish, the birds, and every living creature. I give you every seed-bearing plant and fruit for your food. And I give every green plant for food to the living creatures on the land and in the air." God brought the animals and birds to Adam and told him to name them. So Adam gave them names. Was the first man a cave man who could only grunt? No way! He was super smart. All of God's creation was perfect. The Bible says that when God looked at it, He saw that it was good.

HOW THIS ANIMAL TALE CAN HELP YOU

The Bible account of creation is absolutely true. Not everyone believes this, though. If you believe the Bible, some people may make fun of you. What will you do then? Here are some suggestions:

1. First, have faith in God. *By faith we understand that the universe was formed at God's command, so that what is seen was not made out of what was visible.* (Hebrews 11:2). Faith is taking God at His word and acting on it. God said He created all things. By faith, stand up and be counted on God's side. Don't let others shake your faith.

2. If you are God's child, His Holy Spirit lives in you. He will help you answer those who don't believe in God.

3. Read and study the Bible to learn more about God and His creation. This book of devotions will help you, too. As you read these true tales about animals, remember that the Bible says God made them. Believe it!

⊢WHO DID IT⊣

Through him all things were made; without him nothing was made that has been made. John 1:3. Through whom were all things made? Solve the puzzle below to find the answer. The pictures show some things the Creator made. Write the name of each picture in the boxes beside it. Then write the letters below the numbers on these blank lines in order:

___ ___ ___ ___ ___ ___ ___ ___ ___ ___ ___ made all things.

What is His name? On the lines, write the letter that follows the one given below it:

His name is ___ ___ ___ ___ ___.
          I   D   R   T   R

2
A Snake Causes Big Trouble in the Garden

"Now the serpent was more crafty than any of the wild animals the Lord God had made."

—Genesis 3:1

The first animal in a Bible story is a serpent (a snake). It let Satan use it. The Bible calls Satan "the great dragon" and "that ancient serpent." Where did he come from? Was he always such a terrible creature? Satan was once Lucifer, the most beautiful and wise of all God's angels.

Lucifer became proud and decided he wanted to be like God. He wanted the worship that only God deserves. He influenced many other angels to follow him. God knew what was going on, and he cast Lucifer and his followers out of heaven. They became Satan (the devil) and the demons.

Satan hates God, so he tried to tempt the very first people to disobey God. He used a snake to help him do it.

ANIMAL FACTS
⊢SNAKES⊣

Why wasn't Eve afraid of the snake in this story? When God created all animals, they were good. There was nothing about the snake to make Eve afraid.

When God first made snakes, were they poisonous? Did they bite people? No. Animals did not hurt each other or man in the beginning.

Did snakes eat other animals? No. God provided grasses and plants as food for all land animals in the beginning.

When did snakes become dangerous to people and to other animals? Look for the answer to this question in the Bible animal tale.

Did the snake in the story wriggle along the ground? Probably not. The first snakes may have walked upright. Now discover when they began to crawl on their bellies.

BIBLE ANIMAL TALE
⊢A CRAFTY SNAKE TEMPTS
THE FIRST WOMAN⊣
(GENESIS 3:1–19)

A beautiful, cunning creature—a snake—moved through the Garden of Eden. He came up to Eve in a friendly sort of way. Eve wasn't afraid of him. She had no reason to be. No animal in the garden had ever harmed her.

Then the snake began to speak. (Actually, it was Satan, speaking through the snake's mouth.) "Did God really say, 'You must not eat from any tree in the garden'?" the snake asked.

Eve replied, "We may eat fruit from the trees in the garden. But God did tell us not to eat fruit from the tree in the middle of the garden, or we will die." She was talking about the tree of the knowledge of good and evil.

"Oh, no!" the snake said. "You won't die. When you eat the fruit, you will become like God, knowing good and evil."

Eve looked at the fruit. It is beautiful, she thought. *It must be very delicious, and it will make me wise.* So she took some fruit and ate it. She found Adam and gave him some, and he ate it, too. These two people, who had always been good before that, were now sinners.

Adam and Eve hid behind some trees, but God saw them. Because of their sin they had to leave the beautiful garden. Troubles, disasters, sickness, pain, and death began. Weeds, thorns, and thistles grew up in the ground. People had to work hard to make it produce food.

The animal world changed, too. Many animals were no longer friendly to other animals or people. Some became meat eaters, and they hunted other animals and ate them. A few animals even attacked people and hurt or killed them. Sin brought a curse on the whole world.

God told the serpent it would now crawl on its belly and eat dust. This was its punishment for letting Satan use it. Ever since then, snakes wriggle across the ground on their bellies. Also, some snakes poison people.

And what about Satan? One day in the future, he will be thrown into the lake of fire, called *hell.* There he will suffer forever.

HOW THIS ANIMAL TALE CAN HELP YOU

The entire world changed when Adam and Eve sinned. The worst thing was that they now had sinful natures; they had a desire to sin by disobeying God. They passed this nature on to their descendants. Every human being is born with this sinful nature and chooses to sin.

After Adam and Eve sinned, Satan thought all people would be his. He was wrong. Jesus came into the world and died on the cross. He took the punishment for our sins. He was buried, but He rose again in three days. All who believe in Jesus as Savior will go to heaven when they die or when Jesus comes again. Have you believed in Jesus?

⊢FIND SOME ANIMAL TALE WORDS⊣

Below is a list of words taken from this Bible animal tale. Find and circle these words in the word search puzzle. You may go down, across, or diagonally.

BEAUTIFUL	CUNNING	CREATURE	DELICIOUS
SUFFERING	WRIGGLE	GOD	ADAM
SATAN	TREE	GOOD	HIM
SNAKE	WORK	WISE	FRUIT
PAIN	MUST	CRAWL	BELLY
HID	DUST	EDEN	POISON
AFRAID	GARDEN	GRIEF	SHE
NOT	ATE	EVE	DIE
USE			

X	G	A	D	A	M	D	C	X	M	D
B	E	A	U	T	I	F	U	L	U	E
E	D	F	R	U	I	T	N	S	S	L
L	E	R	C	D	I	E	N	X	T	I
L	N	A	H	R	E	W	I	S	E	C
Y	G	I	T	I	A	N	N	E	C	I
X	O	D	X	E	M	W	G	V	R	O
X	D	W	R	I	G	G	L	E	E	U
S	U	F	F	E	R	I	N	G	A	S
N	A	X	P	O	I	S	O	N	T	W
A	O	T	R	E	E	H	U	X	U	O
K	X	T	A	X	F	E	I	S	R	R
E	P	A	I	N	G	O	O	D	E	K

3
GOD LIKES ABEL'S LAMB

Do not be like Cain, who belonged to the evil one and murdered his brother. And why did he murder him? Because his own actions were evil and his brother's were righteous.
—1 John 3:12

It's hard to believe, but it's true. The firstborn son of Adam and Eve murdered his brother. It happened after Cain and Abel brought offerings to God.

All through Old Testament times, people gave offerings to God. Most of these were animal sacrifices. Usually, a sacrifice involved killing an animal. Why was this done? The facts about sacrifices in this devotion will help you understand animal sacrifices better.

ANIMAL FACTS
ᚼANIMAL SACRIFICESᚼ

When did animal sacrifices begin? The Bible doesn't tell us the exact time. We know that when Adam and Eve sinned, they realized that they were naked. They tried to make some coverings for themselves with fig leaves. After God put them out of the garden, He made garments of skin for them to wear for clothing.

Where did God get the skins? God either killed some animals or had Adam do it. Either way, animals had to die so that people could be covered. Perhaps right then God taught Adam and Eve that blood must be shed to cover over their sins. They learned to bring a sin offering to God of an animal whose blood had been shed.

Why did God want that kind of sacrifice? Because it foreshadowed the time when Jesus, the Lamb of God, shed His blood on the cross. There He died for the sins of the world.

Could people sacrifice any kind of animal they chose to bring? No. God told people the exact kind of offerings He wanted. It must be domestic animals—sheep, goats, cows, bulls, or oxen. Each animal must have nothing wrong with it. Why? Because the animal sacrifices represented Jesus, who was absolutely perfect.

Why don't Christians sacrifice animals today? The animal sacrifices in the Old Testament looked forward to the time when Jesus would die for our sins. After He died on the cross and rose again, there was no need for animal sacrifices. When we believe in Him, his blood washes away our sins.

BIBLE ANIMAL TALE
⊢MURDERED FOR OFFERING A LAMB⊣
(GENESIS 4:1–16)

Flocks of sheep peacefully grazed in the fields, watched over by their shepherd, Abel. Not far away, Abel's brother Cain worked the soil of his garden. All was well, until one dreadful day when these brothers brought offerings to God.

Cain and Abel were the first people born in the world. Adam and Eve must have taught their boys about God. "Don't sin," they probably warned their sons.

"God hates sin. Our sin got us and all mankind in trouble." Then Adam most likely told Cain and Abel about bringing an animal sacrifice to God when they did wrong.

When the two boys grew up, Cain chose to be a farmer. He liked to work the soil and grow things. Abel became a shepherd and kept flocks of sheep.

One day Cain and Abel each brought an offering to God. Cain knew the kind of offering God wanted, but he didn't choose to bring a bloody animal. Instead, he brought some things he had grown. Abel killed a lamb from his flock and offered it to God.

Somehow, God showed that He liked Abel's offering. Maybe He sent a fire to burn up the animal sacrifice. Whatever it was, Cain knew that God did not accept the offering he brought. Cain grew very angry, and his face showed it.

"Why are you angry?" God asked Cain. "You can still bring the right kind of offering." But Cain didn't do it.

Cain said to Abel, "Let's go out in the field." When they were there, Cain killed his brother. It was the world's first murder.

God said to Cain, "Where is your brother?"

"I don't know," lied Cain. "Am I supposed to watch over my brother?"

"The voice of your brother's blood cries to me from the ground," God told Cain. "Now you can no longer work the ground and get food from it. You will be a restless wanderer over the earth."

"My punishment is more than I can bear!" cried Cain.

HOW THIS ANIMAL TALE CAN HELP YOU

Abel obeyed God and brought the right kind of offering. Bringing a bloody lamb showed that he wanted God to forgive his sin. God accepted his offering, so we know that He forgave Abel's sins.

God told Cain He would give him a second chance to bring the right offering. Still, Cain refused to bring a lamb and kill it. God did not forgive his sins.

We, too, have a choice to make. Jesus said, "I am the way, the truth, and the life. No one comes to the Father except through me." All persons have sinned. Jesus became the sacrifice for our sins when He died on the cross. He didn't stay dead, though. He came back to life on the third day.

Now the Bible tells us, "Believe in the Lord Jesus Christ, and you will be saved." Have you received Jesus as your sacrifice for your sins? If not, would you like to do so? *(See the last page of this book.)*

⊢WHICH ANIMAL WAS JESUS LIKE?⊣

Long before Jesus came to earth, Isaiah prophesied that He would come to be the Savior who takes away sin. In Isaiah 53:7, he says that Jesus would be like a certain kind of animal. To find which one it was, follow each line, and begining with number 1, write the letters in the order as they appear. After you do the puzzle, read all of Isaiah 53:7.

—— —— —— —— —— —— —— —— —— —— —— —— —— —— —— ——
    1   2   3   4

—— —— —— —— —— —— —— —— —— —— —— —— —— —— —— ——
    5   6   7   8

—— —— —— —— —— —— —— —— —— ——.
              9

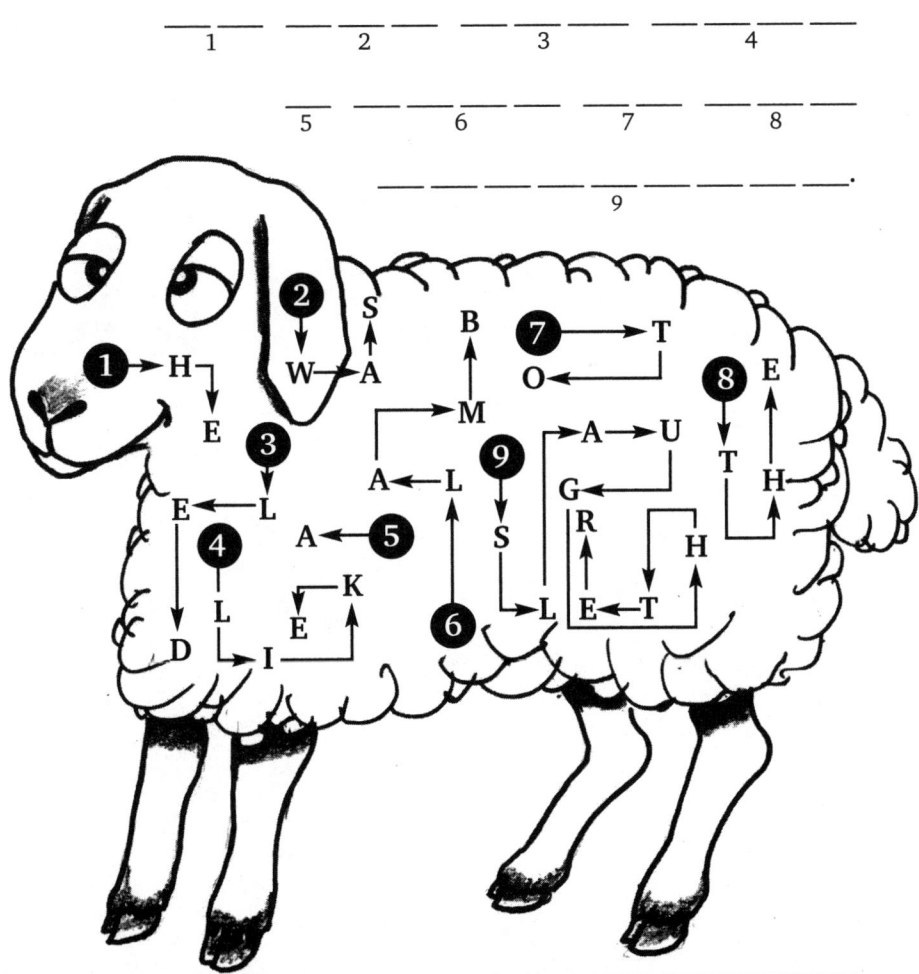

4
THE ANIMALS WHO SURVIVED THE GREAT FLOOD

"Pairs of clean and unclean animals, of birds and of all creatures that move along the ground, male and female, came to Noah and entered the ark."
—Genesis &:8-9

What a sight! Animals came to Noah from everywhere. There were more different kinds of animals than in the largest zoo. In fact, every kind of living bird and land animal came to Noah, preparing to enter the ark.

Some people don't believe the story about the Great Flood. They say the story has to be untrue. Here are some facts that Bible-believing scientists and teachers have given us to answer the questions of such people.

ANIMAL FACTS
⊢THE ANIMALS ON THE ARK⊣

Did Noah travel all over the world to find these animals and bring them to the ark? No. God told Noah that all the animals would come to him.

How did the animals know where to go? God sent the animals to Noah. Since God made the animals, He knows how to communicate with them. Animals also understand what God says to them. In the Bible, everytime God gave a command to an animal, it obeyed.

How could all these animals fit into the ark? The boat Noah made by God's instructions was 450 feet long, 75 feet wide, and 45 feet high. It had three decks, with a total area of 101,250 feet, each fitted with rooms or stalls. These could easily have handled about 125,000 animals. It is estimated that not more than 35,000 animals were on the ark.

What kept them from fighting each other and eating each other up? When the animals settled down in their stalls, God might have caused them to go into a period of hibernation. However He did it, we know God kept them all alive.

Where did the animals get food to eat? God told Noah to take every kind of food and to store it away for people and animals. There was enough room on the ark for both the animals and their food.

Which animals were clean and which were unclean? The clean animals were those that could be sacrificed. All the others were called unclean.

BIBLE ANIMAL TALE
⊢A HUGE BOATLOAD OF ANIMALS⊣
(GENESIS 6–8)

Outside a huge boat, every kind of animal waited to go inside. Only the water creatures that could swim were not there. Noah and his sons had been building that boat, called an ark, for 120 years.

The Lord had seen how great man's wickedness on the earth had become. Noah was the only one who pleased God. So one day God said to Noah, "I am going to bring floodwaters on the earth to destroy all life. Make yourself an ark of cypress wood. Then you and your family will go inside it."

God told Noah exactly how to build the boat. He also told him to take one pair of each kind of unclean animal and seven pairs of clean animals inside it. At last, everything was ready. Then God said to Noah, "Go into the ark, you and your whole family, because you are righteous. Also take the animals in with you."

Noah, his family, and all the animals went into the ark. Then God shut the door. After seven days, rain began to fall. Noah and his family must have been amazed. It had never rained before. Also, waters gushed up from beneath the ground. It rained for 40 days and 40 nights.

Floodwaters covered the whole earth, even the highest mountains. The ark rode on top of the water, keeping all on board safe. Every other living thing on the land drowned. The waters flooded the earth for 150 days.

Then the waters began to go down. Finally, the ark rested on a high mountaintop. What happened to the people and animals? Find out in the next devotion.

HOW THIS ANIMAL TALE CAN HELP YOU

It must have been dark and a little scary in the ark. Noah and his family knew a terrible catastrophe was about to happen. For seven days, they sat there, waiting. No one could get out, because God had shut the door.

Suddenly, they heard the strange sound of raindrops on the roof. Water gushed up from the earth. There must have been all kinds of strange noises. Before long, the ark rode on top of floodwaters. Were Noah and his family scared? They didn't need to be. Someone else was inside that ark. God rode the waters with them. He protected them and brought them out safely.

When you have scary times, remember that your Heavenly Father is there with you. He loves you and has promised to take care of you. Bad times do happen to all of us, but God will help us and do what is best for us. We can say, "When I am afraid, I will trust in you" (Psalm 56:3). Remember this the next time you are frightened.

PEOPLE AND ANIMALS MATCH UP

In the word list below are the names of some of the animals that survived the Great Flood. These kinds of animals are in other stories in this book, also. Fit these names into the puzzle blanks. Then answer the question below the puzzle by writing, in order, the letters already printed in the blanks.

GOAT   DOVE   CAMEL   SNAKE
HORSE   LAMB   SHEEP   MULE
DONKEY   LION   DOG   PIG

1.   C ___ ___ ___ ___

2.   ___ ___ R ___ ___

3.   ___ ___ E ___ ___

4.   ___ ___ A ___ ___

5.   ___ ___ ___ T ___

6.   ___ ___ ___ E ___

7.   D ___ ___ ___

8.   ___ ___ ___ B ___

9.   ___ ___ ___ ___ ___ Y ___

10.   ___ ___ G ___

11.   ___ ___ O ___

12.   D ___ ___

What do all these animals have in common? They were all

___ ___ ___ ___ ___ ___ ___ ___ ___ ___ ___ ___ .

5
TWO BIRD MESSENGERS

"After forty days Noah opened the window he had made in the ark and sent out a raven.... Then he sent out a dove."
—Genesis 8:6-8

How long ago was the first mail delivered by air? Fifty years? One hundred years? One thousand years? Actually, mail was delivered by air about three thousand years ago. It's true that the first airplane flight was in 1903. But the first carrier of mail by air was not a plane. It was a bird.

Birds similar to homing pigeons were probably the first carriers of "air mail." The Egyptians used pigeons to carry written messages at least 3,000 years ago. In this Bible story, a raven and a dove gave messages to Noah—not in writing, but by their actions.

ANIMAL FACTS
⊢RAVENS AND DOVES⊣

According to the *Encyclopedia Britannica*, there are between 10,000 and 12,000 known species of birds. There are over 350 different kinds of birds in Israel today. Of these, 26 are found there and nowhere else. The Bible mentions birds about 300 times and gives the names of about 34 birds.

⊢RAVENS⊣

What are ravens like?   A raven is a member of the crow family. It has a larger head and shoulders than crows do. It may sometimes be 26 inches long. Its wings may spread out as wide as three feet. The gray raven, with gray and black feathers, is a native of Israel.

What do ravens eat? Ravens are scavengers; they will eat almost anything. They feed on both animal and vegetable matter and can live on dead bodies.

⊢DOVES⊣

What are doves like? Doves are in the same family as pigeons. Usually, the Bible doesn't distinguish between doves and pigeons.

What do doves look like? A dove is a small, trim bird. There are a number of different kinds of doves. The turtledove, mentioned in the Bible, has ash-gray plumage, tinged with red. It is a shy bird.

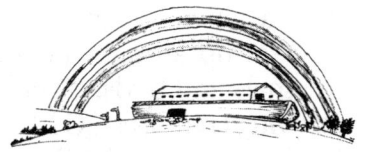

ANIMAL BIBLE TALE
⊢TWO BIRDS FLY OUT THE WINDOW⊣
(GENESIS 8:1⊢12)

Noah opened the window of the ark and let a raven out. Away it went, flapping its wings. How happy it must have been to fly freely after being cooped up for a year! It found places to land. Perhaps it perched on floating logs or other debris. There were plenty of dead carcasses it could eat. So the raven flew back and forth over the land, but it did not return to Noah.

When the raven did not return, Noah knew that the waters had gone down some. Then Noah sent out a dove. He knew that the gentle, timid dove would help him know what the conditions outside were like. Before long, it flew back to Noah in the ark. Noah reached out his hand and brought it back into the ark. *It couldn't find a place to land,* Noah thought. The lowlands must still be flooded.

After seven days, Noah sent the dove out again. In the evening, it returned. This time it had an olive leaf in its mouth. *Good! The valleys where the olive trees grow are dry,* Noah decided. Noah waited seven more days and sent the dove out again. This time it did not return. Noah knew it had found a comfortable place to spend the night.

Later, Noah removed the covering from the ark and looked out. The water was gone! It was almost time for the family to leave the ark. When the ground was dry, God said to Noah, "Come out of the ark, you and your family, and bring out all the animals."

Noah, his family, and the animals came out of the ark 371 days after entering it. He set up an altar of rocks and sacrificed some of the clean animals and birds. "I will never again send a flood to destroy all living creatures," God promised Noah. He put a rainbow in the sky as a reminder that He would keep His promise.

⊢How This Animal Tale Can Help You⊣

By their actions, the raven and the dove sent messages to Noah. They helped him know when the ground was dry. Then he could safely take his family and the animals out of the ark.

God spoke directly to Noah and gave him many messages, such as these:

• Build a boat by the directions I give you.
• Go into the boat with your family. Take pairs of all animals with you.
• Come out of the ark.

Noah paid attention to God's messages and obeyed Him.

Do you receive messages from God? Yes. He wrote the entire Bible to give us His messages. Also, Christians have the Holy Spirit living inside. He speaks to us in our minds and hearts to help us understand God's messages. Our part is to read the Bible, pay attention to what God says, and obey Him.

Take time to read God's messages. Obey them. You will never regret these actions.

⊢TWO MESSAGES
FROM GOD⊣

To discover two messages from God to Noah about floodwaters, use the code to fill the blanks.

A=1	B=2	C=3	D=4
E=5	F=6	H=7	I=8
K=9	L=10	M=11	N=12
O=13	R=14	S=15	T=16
V=17	W=18	Y=19	

All people on the ___ ___ ___ ___ ___ were very
        5 1 14 16 7

___ ___ ___ ___ ___ ___ except ___ ___ ___ ___
18 8 3 9 5 4   12 13 1 7
and his family. God told Noah, "I am going to

___ ___ ___ ___
15 5 12 4

___ ___ ___ ___ ___ ___ ___ ___ ___ ___ to
6 10 13 13 4 18 1 16 5 14 15

___ ___ ___ ___ ___ ___ ___ ___ ___ ___
4 5 15 16 14 13 19   1 10 10

___ ___ ___ ___." God told Noah to build an ark. He, his
10 8 6 5
family, and the animals on board the ark were safe. After the

flood, God put a rainbow in the sky and said,

" ___ ___ ___ ___ ___ again
12 5 17 5 14

___ ___ ___ ___ ___ ___ ___
18 8 10 10 16 7 5

___ ___ ___ ___ ___ ___
18 1 16 5 14 15

___ ___ ___ ___ ___ ___ ___
2 5 3 10 11 5 1

___ ___ ___ ___ ___ to
6 10 13 13 4

___ ___ ___ ___ ___ ___ ___ ___ ___ ___
4 5 15 16 14 13 19 1 10 10

___ ___ ___ ___."
10 8 6 5

6
THE CREATOR DESCRIBES SOME STRANGE ANIMALS

"The wings of the ostrich flap joyfully. Look at the behemoth, which I made along with you. Can you pull in a leviathan with a hook?"
—Job 39:13; 40:15; 41:1

This Bible animal tale will help us understand our troubles a little better. In it, Job wonders why he has troubles. Wow! His troubles were gross! God gave Job an answer as He described some animals, including ostriches, behemoths, and leviathans.

"It's not fair. Why do I have to be sick today?" complains Jennifer. "I worked hard to be the best speller in the state spelling contest. I studied while other kids played. I won our school contest hands down. Now, on the day of the contest I can't go. Why did God let this happen to me?"

Don't we all ask questions like that sometimes? We may never know the answers to some questions. But we can be sure that God is always in control and works all things for good.

ANIMAL FACTS
⊢OSTRICHES, BEHEMOTHS, AND LEVIATHANS⊣

⊢OSTRICHES⊣

To what family does the ostrich belong? It is a strange-looking member of the bird family. At seven to eight feet tall, it is the largest living bird. In Bible times, ostriches were a common sight in the deserts of Israel and Sinai.

Can such a huge bird fly? No, but it can run fast. At top speed, it will cover at least 15 feet in one step and can outrun a horse. Sometimes it will use its wings as a sail to gain greater speed.

Do ostriches have good sense? The ostrich's eye is bigger than its brain. With a brain the size of a walnut, the ostrich is not very bright. "For God did not endow her with wisdom or give her a share of good sense." Job 39:17

⊢BEHEMOTHS⊣

What is a behemoth? The behemoth was a large land animal. No one is sure what it was; but because of its size, it could have been a dinosaur-type animal.

God's description of the behemoth in Job 40:15 sounds a lot like a large sauropod, a kind of dinosaur. Another idea is that the behemoth could have been a hippopotamus. These animals can submerge themselves in water and can also live on land. (Read about a behemoth in Job 40:15-24.) What do you think a behemoth might have been?

⊣LEVIATHANS⊢

What is a leviathan? (Read about a leviathan in Job 41:1-34.) A leviathan was a great water creature, probably a kind of dinosaur. Another suggestion is that it could have been a crocodile or a whale.

BIBLE ANIMAL TALE
⊢GOD TEACHES JOB A LESSON
FROM THE ANIMALS⊣
(JOB 1–2; 40:15–24; 16:1–34; 42:7–15)

Job was in big trouble. "I wish I had never been born!" he said. He and his three friends discussed why people suffer. God answered them by reminding them of His great power in creation. He even used some animals to teach Job a lesson.

Job was a good man who loved God. Job was very rich. He had 7,000 sheep, 3,000 camels, 1,000 oxen, and 500 donkeys. He had a wife, seven sons, three daughters, and many servants.

Satan asked God to let him bring trouble to Job, and God agreed. Robbers stole Job's oxen and donkeys and killed many of his servants. Fire came from the sky and burned up his sheep and more servants. Three raiding parties carried all of his camels away. While Job's children dined, a strong wind blew their house down around them, killing them. Last of all, Satan caused Job to have painful sores all over his body. *Why do I have so many troubles?* Job wondered.

Three of Job's friends told him, "Your troubles must have come because you have sinned," they said. Job didn't know of any bad thing in his life. He said, "Let God answer me and tell me what I did wrong."

Finally, God spoke to Job and his friends from a whirlwind. He didn't tell Job why bad things had happened. He just reminded Job of His great wisdom and power in creating the earth and all things in it. God wanted Job to know that He is always in control and does what is best.

God talked about some of the animals He had created. He asked Job if he could create such animals. Job knew, of course, that he couldn't do that.

Job didn't ask God "why" anymore. He knew that God was in control and that's all he needed to know. Job told God, "I despise myself and repent in dust and ashes." Then God gave Job twice as much as he had before: 14,000 sheep, 6,000 camels 2,000 oxen, and 1,000 donkeys. He also gave him another seven sons and three daughters. Job was very rich, indeed!

How This Animal Tale Can Help You

God created and controls the heavens, the earth, and all of nature. He is wise enough and powerful enough to be in charge of us, too. Sometimes God allows bad things to happen in our lives. We get sick or hurt. A loved one dies. We lose the things we own. All of these troubles came to Job. They didn't happen because Job was bad; he was a good man.

Job learned that nothing is out of God's control. God has reasons for allowing our troubles. Sometimes we'll find out why, but not always. The important thing is to trust God. When troubles come, tell Him how you feel. Ask Him to make you strong enough to go through your hard times. Remember, God is in control. He's all you need!

⊢MATCH THEM UP⊣

The animals that God talked to Job about are listed on the left column below. A description about each animal is listed in the right column. Draw lines to match each animal with its description.

1. Lion

2. Raven

3. Mountain goat

4. Wild donkey

5. Ostrich

6. Horse

7. Hawk

8. Eagle

9. Behemoth

10. Leviathan

A. A small animal, similar to the horse, with large ears

B. Could have been a land dinosaur or a hippopotamus

C. A large black bird in the crow family

D. A large, solid-hoofed animal that is ridden and can be raced

E. Probably a water dinosaur or a crocodile.

F. A very large bird that makes its nest in high places

G. Similar to a sheep, but with horns

H. A large animal of the cat family

I. A bird of prey that catches living animals and kills them

J. The largest bird

7
THE RAM CAUGHT IN THE THICKET

"Abraham looked up and there in a thicket he saw a ram caught by its horns."

—Genesis 22:13

Suppose you had a brother, a sister, or a friend who stole something from you. Then this person was caught with the goods. For punishment, he or she would be grounded for a week. No television, games, or other fun things would be allowed.

What would you do? Would you say to this person, "Good! You deserve every bit of that punishment. I hope you're miserable all week!" Or would you say, "I know you stole from me, but I love you. I will take your punishment for you. I will be grounded for a week, with no fun things to do."

Most people would do the first thing. After all, it would be fair for that person to suffer for stealing from you. Instead, suppose you did the second thing. Wow! You'd really have to love a person to do that!

Stop and think a minute. Someone showed that kind of love to you. You sinned against Him, yet He took your punishment by dying on the cross. If you believe in Him, He will take your sins away and will never punish you for them. Who loves you that much? Of course you know He's Jesus. He became your substitute and died in your place.

In this Bible story, an animal became a substitute. It was a ram.

ANIMAL FACTS
⊢RAMS⊣

What is a ram? A ram is a male sheep.

Are sheep mentioned often in the Bible? Yes, more times than any other animal.

Were sheep important to the people of the Bible? Yes. Being a shepherd was an important occupation. Sheep's milk, meat, and wool provided people with food and clothing. The horns were used as trumpets or for carrying oil. A very important use for sheep was in sacrifices.

Were all sheep domestic animals in Bible times? No. Wild sheep, called rams or mountain sheep, lived in the hill country.

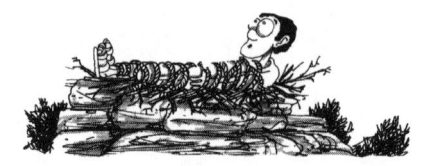

BIBLE ANIMAL TALE
⊢A RAM SUBSTITUTE FOR ISAAC⊣
(GENESIS 22:1-19)

A ram walked on a mountain in the land of Moriah. He tried to go through a thick clump of bushes, but his horns got caught. Probably he struggled hard, but he couldn't get out of those bushes. He was not there by chance. The Lord had caused him to be there.

God had said to Abraham, "Take your son, your only son, Isaac, whom you love and go to the land of Moriah. Sacrifice Isaac there as a burnt offering on a mountain I will tell you about."

Isaac was very special to Abraham. Long before, God had promised to give a son to Abraham. He would be the beginning of a great nation of God's people, the Hebrews. Abraham believed God, but he waited and waited. Finally, when Abraham was 100 years old, Isaac was born. Of course Isaac was special!

Abraham didn't ask any questions. He obeyed God. The next morning he saddled his donkey and cut wood for the offering. He started for the mountain, taking with him two servants and Isaac.

When Abraham saw the mountain in the distance, he stopped. He told his servants, "Stay here with the donkey while I and the boy go over there. We will worship and then we will come back to you."

Abraham placed the wood on Isaac, and he carried the fire and the knife. As they walked, Isaac asked, "Father, the fire and the wood are here, but where is the lamb for the offering?"

"God will provide an offering," Abraham said. They walked to the mountain. "Here we are," Abraham said. He built an altar and arranged the wood on it. He bound Isaac and laid him on the wood. Next, he raised the knife to kill his son.

"Abraham! Abraham! Don't lay a hand on the boy," God said. "Now I know you fear God."

Then Abraham looked up. There was a ram, caught in the bushes by its horns! He got the ram loose from the bushes and sacrificed it instead of his son.

⊢HOW THIS ANIMAL TALE CAN HELP YOU⊣

Did Abraham love God? Yes, he loved God more than anything—even more than his special son. God tested him by telling him to sacrifice Isaac. Abraham passed the test when he raised his knife to kill him. At that moment, God provided a sacrifice—the ram in the bushes. The ram was Isaac's substitute.

All people have sinned. God hates sin, and sinners must be punished. But God loves all people. He doesn't want anyone to be punished. That's why He sent His only Son into the world. Jesus loved us so much that He willingly died on the cross for our sins. He took our punishment and became our Substitute.

Jesus didn't stay dead, though. He rose again on the third day. Now all who believe in Him will be saved. He will forgive our sins and make us His children. Do you want to receive Jesus, your Substitute, as your Savior? *(See the last page.)*

⊢JESUS, OUR SUBSTITUTE.
CROSSWORD PUZZLE⊣

In this puzzle, there are four names for the Son of God:

LORD   The ever-living God in heaven.
JESUS   The One who came to earth to save His people
            from their sins.
CHRIST   The Messiah, whom God promised in the Old
            Testament to send to earth.
SAVIOR   Our Substitute who died on the cross.

Beside the puzzle are pictures of objects that were connected
with Jesus' life on earth. Fill in the crossword puzzle with the
missing words.

8
CAMELS BRING
A BRIDE FOR ISAAC

"Then Rebekah and her maids got ready and mounted their camels and went back with the man."
—Genesis 24:61

A car comes up to a crossroad. The driver looks both ways but sees no signs. "Hmmm. I don't know which way to go," he says. "I guess I'll just drive straight ahead. This must be the way."

"There's a service station. We'd better stop and ask the way," says the driver's wife. But the driver travels on, not asking for help or looking at a map. He doesn't know it, but he is traveling farther and farther from his destination.

Does this sound foolish? You bet! What is more foolish, though, is when we make decisions in life without asking for directions. The man in this animal tale asked for directions from the right person. He rode on a camel, the "ship of the desert," as they are sometimes called.

ANIMAL FACTS
⊢CAMELS⊣

Do camels carry water in their humps? No. The hump, weighing up to 80 pounds or more, doesn't carry water, although camels can go for weeks without water. The hump is filled with fat, which helps the camel go for a long time without food.

How can a camel go without water for a long time? Its body can tolerate a much higher body temperature than humans, allowing it to retain water, even though the air is very hot.

How can a camel stand the glare of the bright sun and sandstorms of the desert? Its eyes are protected by three sets of overhanging lids and by long eyelashes. Its bushy eyebrows help keep sand out of its eyes, too. Its nostrils can be closed up tight against the driving sand of the desert storms.

How tall are camels? How can people climb on board them? Camels usually stand six feet or more at the shoulder. They are trained to kneel to take on a load. Their chest and knees have horny pads that protect them from the sand when they kneel.

What do camels eat? Almost anything. They can eat and digest bitter thorny shrubs and many other things

BIBLE ANIMAL TALE
⊢THE CAMELS ARE COMING!⊣
(GENESIS 24:1–66)

A herd of ten camels plodded over the desert sands. Abraham's chief servant and other men rode on them. The men were on a mission for Abraham.

One day Abraham had called his chief servant to him. "Make me a solemn promise in the name of God," he said. "Promise you will go to my country and my relatives and find a wife for Isaac. Bring her here. Do not take Isaac to that country. If the woman will not come with you, I release you from your promise."

The chief servant promised Abraham he would go. He got out ten of his master's camels. He and other servants rode on some of them. The other camels carried all kinds of good gifts from Abraham.

After many days, the travelers reached Nahor, where some of Abraham's relatives lived. The servant had the camels kneel down near the well outside town. It was evening, the time when the women from the town came to get water.

The servant prayed, "O Lord God of my master Abraham, give me good success. Show kindness to my master. The girls will soon come to draw water. I will ask a girl to let down her jar that I may have a drink. If she says, 'Drink, and I'll water your camels too,' may she be the one You have chosen for Isaac."

Before he finished praying, Rebekah came out with her jar on her shoulder. She was very beautiful. She went to the spring and filled her jar. The servant asked her for a drink.

"Drink, my lord," she said. She lowered the jar and gave him a drink. Then she said, "I'll draw water for all your camels, too." The servant watched her closely, as she kept drawing water until all the camels were satisfied.

This is the girl, the servant decided. He took out a gold ring and two gold bracelets and gave them to the girl. "Whose daughter are you?" he asked. "Is there room in your father's house for us to spend the night?"

"I am the daughter of Bethuel, the son of Nahor," she said. "We have plenty of straw and fodder for your camels and room for you to spend the night."

The servant bowed down and worshiped God. "Praise be to the Lord, Who has shown kindness to my master," he said. The girl was a granddaughter of his master's brother!

When they arrived at Rebekah's house, the servant told her family why he had come. He gave Abraham's gifts to the family. "Will you let Rebekah go back with me?" he asked. Her father and brother gave their permission, and Rebecca agreed to go.

Isaac went out to his field one evening. He looked at a cloud of dust in the distance. "The camels are coming!" he said. When Rebekah saw Isaac, she quickly covered her face with a thin veil and went to meet him. The servant told Isaac what had happened. Isaac married Rebekah, and he loved her very much.

⸞How This Animal Tale Can Help You⸞

Abraham's chief servant made a long trip to keep a promise. Finding the right girl wouldn't be easy. He didn't try to figure this out by himself, though. He asked God about it. Only God knows all things, and He could help the servant. We don't have to make decisions by ourselves.

We can have God's help. "If any of you lacks wisdom, he should ask God, who gives generously to all without finding fault, and it will be given to him. But when he asks, he must believe and not doubt" (James 1:5, 6). When you truly want to do God's will, ask Him to help you know what to do. Believe Him to do it, and He will. That's for sure!

⸞Who Will Help You Know God's Will?⸞

Unscramble the mixed-up words and write one letter in each box. Look up the Bible verse to find a word, if necessary. Write the numbered letters in scrambled order and then unscramble them to answer the question at the bottom of the page. (The numbers over the squares show whether the letters are in the first or second word.)

		2		1			
Don't quit	G	I	R	A	N	P	Y

—1 Thessalonians 5:17

		1		1	
Call upon the Lord	I	L	D	A	Y

—Psalm 88:9

	1		2		2
Search for God with all your	E	R	A	T	H

—Jeremiah 29:13

			1		1
Ask, and it shall be	V	I	N	E	G

—Matthew 7:7

	2				2
Have	H	A	F	I	T

—Hebrews 11:6

		1			2		1
When you pray,	E	B	E	V	I	E	L

—Mark 11:24

Write the scrambled letters here:

1___ ___ ___ ___ ___ ___ ___ ___

2___ ___ ___ ___ ___ ___

Who Will Help You Know God's Will?

Our ___ ___ ___ ___ ___ ___ ___ ___

___ ___ ___ ___ ___ ___

9
GRAB A SNAKE
BY ITS TAIL

"Then the Lord said to him, 'Reach out your hand and take it by the tail.' So Moses reached out and took hold of the snake and it turned back into a staff in his hand."
—Genesis 3:1

Do you like snakes? Some snakes have pretty markings. Snakes are graceful as they glide over the ground. Only about eight out of a hundred snakes are poisonous to people. But one bite from a poisonous snake could kill a person.

If someone challenged you to grab a snake by its tail, would you do it? Maybe you would, if you knew it was non-poisonous. But would you grab a snake by its tail if you didn't know it was harmless? Its tail is not dangerous, but its other end might be. If you grabbed its tail, it might whip around and bite you.

In this Bible animal tale, God asked Moses to do a hard thing. He used a snake to show Moses that He had the power to help him do it.

ANIMAL FACTS
⊢SNAKES⊣

How many vertebrae does a snake have? A snake's backbone is a very long chain of up to 300 vertebrae, and each has a pair of ribs attached. Its long backbone helps a snake curve, climb, crawl, and swim.

Why does a snake have scales? They keep the snake's body from losing too much moisture. Also the scales on the underside give it traction.

Does a snake have ears? Its ears can't be seen from the outside, and it is deaf to sound carried by air. It depends on vibrations to pick up sounds.

Do snakes ever close their eyes? No. Transparent eyelids hold the eyes open and protect a snake's eyes.

BIBLE ANIMAL TALE
⊢A STAFF BECOMES A SNAKE⊣
(EXODUS 3:1–20; 4:1–5; 7:8–13)

One day God told Moses to catch a snake by its tail. It happened in the desert, where Moses was taking care of sheep. First, he saw a bush on fire that didn't burn up. Moses came closer to examine the strange sight. Then God spoke to him from within the bush, "Moses! Moses!"

"Here I am," said Moses.

"Don't come any closer," God told him. "You are standing on holy ground. Take off your sandals." Then God continued, "I am the God of your father, the God of Abraham, Isaac, and Jacob." Moses hid his face. He was afraid to look.

"I see the misery of My people in Egypt," God said. "I have heard them cry out because of their slave drivers. You go to Egypt. Bring my people out."

God's people, the Hebrews (also called Israelites), had been in Egypt for a long time. One of their pharaohs (rulers) had made the Hebrews his slaves. Now the present pharaoh and other Egyptians made their lives miserable.

Moses said, "Who am I, that I should go to Pharaoh and bring the Israelites out of Egypt?"

"I will be with you," God told him. "Tell the Israelite leaders that the Lord God has sent you. Tell them I promise to bring them out of their misery. I will bring them to a land flowing with milk and honey. Then you and the leaders go to Pharaoh. Tell him you want to go for a three-day journey into the desert to worship me."

"What if the leaders won't believe me?" asked Moses.

"What do you have in your hand?" God asked.

"A staff," Moses replied.

"Throw it on the ground," the Lord said. Moses threw it on the ground. Zap! It became a snake. The scared Moses ran away fast! "Reach out your hand and take it by the tail," God said. Maybe Moses' hand shook, but he grabbed the snake. Zap! It became a staff again.

"Do this before the leaders, and they will believe you," God told him.

Moses obeyed God and went to Egypt. He and his brother Aaron talked to the leaders. They showed them the miracle of the staff and other miracles. Then the leaders went with Moses to see Pharaoh. The following several devotions will tell what happened next.

⊢HOW THIS ANIMAL TALE CAN HELP YOU⊣

When you grow up, God may want you to serve Him in a difficult place. If He does, remember that God has all power. He'll help you do what He tells you to do.

What does God want you to do right now? The Bible tells you many things you should do. It tells you to obey your parents. It tells you to witness to others about Jesus. It helps you know about good things you should do. It warns you about bad things you shouldn't do.

It isn't always easy to obey God. Others may make fun of you or try to stop you from doing right. The wonderful thing is that our God has the power to help us do right. If you put Him first, He will help you do the right things. Both now and in your future life, don't be afraid to do what God wants.

⊢THE KEY TO
A SUCCESSFUL LIFE⊣

God tells us in Matthew what we need to do first and what needs to be most important in our lives. Use the code below to find what this is.

A=2	B=4	C=6	D=8
E=10	F=12	G=14	H=16
I=18	J=20	K=22	L=24
M=26	N=28	O=30	P=32
Q=34	R=36	S=38	T=40
U=42	V=44	W=46	X=48
Y=50	Z=52		

＿＿ ＿＿ ＿＿ ＿＿   ＿＿ ＿＿ ＿＿ ＿＿ ＿＿   ＿＿ ＿＿ ＿＿ ＿＿ ,
38 10 10 22   12 18 36 38 40   14 30 8   38

＿＿ ＿＿ ＿＿ ＿＿ ＿＿ ＿＿ ＿＿   ＿＿ ＿＿ ＿＿   ＿＿ ＿＿ ＿＿
22 18 28 14 8   30 26   2   28 8   16 18 38

＿＿ ＿＿ ＿＿ ＿＿ ＿＿ ＿＿ ＿＿ ＿＿ ＿＿ ＿＿ ＿＿ ＿＿ ＿＿ .
36 18 14 16 40 10 30 42 38 28 10 38 38

THEN GOD WILL GIVE US ＿＿ ＿＿ ＿＿   ＿＿ ＿＿ ＿＿ ＿＿ ＿＿
2   24 24   40 16 10 38 10

＿＿ ＿＿ ＿＿ ＿＿ ＿＿ ＿＿ THAT WE NEED. (See Matthew 6:33)
40 16 18 28 14 38

10
PLAGUES 1 AND 2 ON EGYPT: BLOOD & FROGS

"The fish in the Nile died, and the river smelled so bad that the Egyptians could not drink its water. And the frogs came up and covered the land."

—Exodus 7:21; 8:6

We can count on it. A harvest follows the planting of seeds. "A man reaps what he sows" (Galatians 6:7). If a farmer sows weeds, will he get a harvest of corn? No, he'll get weeds. A person who sows good deeds reaps a harvest of good results. One who sows evil deeds reaps a harvest of trouble.

God sent Moses to tell Pharaoh he must let the Israelites go. "No. You can't go," Pharaoh said. So God sent ten dreadful plagues on Egypt. This meant trouble big time for Pharaoh and all his people. Pharaoh's harvest time had come.

In the next five devotions, we'll see how these plagues brought terrible trouble to both the people and their animals.

ANIMAL FACTS
⊢FISH & FROGS⊣

⊢FISH⊣

Did fish live in the great Nile River in Egypt? Yes. The Nile supported a large fishing industry. The Egyptians depended on the Nile for their water. When it flooded each year, it left a rich soil behind where farmers harvested many crops. The Nile River was so important that the Egyptians considered it to be a god.

⊢FROGS⊣

Where were most of the frogs in Egypt? When the Nile River went back inside its banks after a flood, it left pools of water. Many frogs were hatched in these pools.

Did the Egyptians worship frogs? Yes, the Egyptians worshiped frogs as the symbol of a goddess.

BIBLE ANIMAL TALE
⊢FISH DIE IN BLOODY WATER AND FROGS INVADE THE LAND⊣
(EXODUS 7:14–24; 8:1–15)

Would you like to drink bloody water? Would you want to have frogs hopping all over your house and you, too? Pharaoh and the Egyptians didn't like these things, but they happened.

Moses and Aaron obeyed God and stood before Pharaoh. They told him, "The God of Israel says, 'Let my people go to hold a festival to Me in the desert.'"

Pharaoh looked down from his throne and snarled, "Who is the Lord, that I should obey Him? I don't know the Lord, and I won't let Israel go."

"The Lord our God may cause plagues to come on the land," warned Moses.

"Make the Israelites work harder," Pharaoh ordered the slave drivers. "They are lazy. Make them gather their own straw to make bricks, and they must make as many bricks as before."

God said to Moses, "Pharaoh goes out to the water each morning. Meet him on the bank of the Nile and take Aaron's staff with you."

When Pharaoh and his officials came to the Nile, Aaron raised his staff. He struck the water of the Nile, and all the water changed into blood. The fish in the Nile died, and the water stunk. The Egyptians and their animals couldn't drink it.

Blood was everywhere in Egypt, even in the wooden buckets and stone jars. But Pharaoh would not let God's people go.

Seven days passed. At God's command, Moses went back to Pharaoh. He told him, "God says, 'Let my people go. If you won't do it, I will send a plague of frogs all over your country."

"No! No! No! You can't go!" Pharaoh shouted. So Aaron stretched out his staff over the waters of Egypt. At once, frogs came up and covered the land.

They hopped into Pharaoh's palace. They invaded his bedroom and his bed. People found them in their ovens, their kitchen containers, and their food. Frogs hopped all over the people.

Pharaoh called for Moses and Aaron. "Pray to the Lord to take the frogs away," he said. "Then I will let your people go."

Moses asked the Lord to take away the frogs, and they died in the houses, courtyards, and fields. People piled them up in stinking heaps. Did Pharaoh let Israel go then? Read the next devotion to find the answer.

⊢How This Animal Tale Can Help You⊣

Pharaoh could have done what God said at once. He would have spared himself and his people from God's punishment. But Pharaoh hadn't learned his lesson yet. Even after the first two plagues, he still refused to obey God. It took eight more plagues before he finally did what God said.

When you're young, it's easy to think about the present only. The future, when you're older, seems to be a long time away. You don't want to think that today's actions may bring consequences later in your life. But God says we'll reap what we sow, and He means it. We'll save ourselves a lot of trouble if we'll remember that.

Your friends may urge you to do something wrong. "Do this just once," they may say. But if you do it once, that can lead to doing it more times. Then, quicker than you think, it's reaping time. "You may be sure that your sin will find you out" (Numbers 32:32). Sow the good stuff now and reap a good harvest later.

⊢REAP A GOOD HARVEST⊣

If you sow the three things listed below, they will help you reap a good harvest in later life. To find what they are, write all the letters with the same shape, in order, in the blanks. For example, fill in the blanks for number 1 with the letter inside each cross. The first letter for each line is done for you.

1. Be 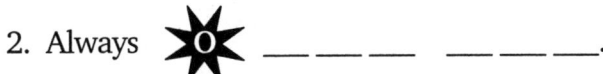 to read the Bible, pray, witness to others and to church.

2. Always  __ __ __ __ __ __.

3. If asked to sin, say,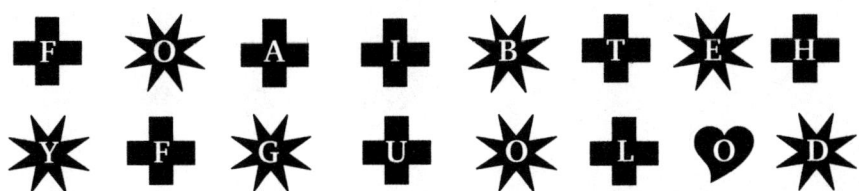

11

PLAGUES 3 AND 4 ON EGYPT: GNATS & FLIES

"All the dust throughout the land of Egypt became gnats. Dense swarms of flies poured into Pharaoh's palace and into the houses of his officials, and throughout Egypt."
—Exodus 8:17, 24

Do you like to watch a magic show? Really there is no magic to it. The so-called magicians do sleight-of-hand tricks or fool people in other ways. It's fun to try to figure out how they do their tricks, but they don't do magic.

Pharaoh had magicians who did mysterious things. The people thought their gods gave the magicians their powers. Actually, the magicians fooled people with trickery or with the help of demons. They were able to perform some things similar to what God did in the first plagues. When God turned dust into gnats, though, the magicians couldn't do that.

The Egyptians had many false gods. Every plague that God sent on Egypt was against one of their gods. This showed the Egyptians that the true God was far more powerful than their false gods.

ANIMAL FACTS
⊢GNATS & FLIES⊣

⊢GNATS⊣

The gnats in the third plague were probably sand flies. Sand flies are tiny insects that suck blood. Their bites are very annoying. Some types of sand flies can cause a virus disease, with fever, headache, and pain in the eyes.

⊢FLIES⊣

There are thousands of different kinds of flies. We don't know for sure which kind God used in the fourth plague. The Bible says God sent swarms of flies, so there may have been more than one kind.

The housefly is a filthy pest. The tiny hairs on its legs carry bacteria that may cause serious diseases. The housefly loves to live in manure piles and garbage. Then it flies into people's homes and leaves germs on dishes and food or even on a person's body.

BIBLE ANIMAL TALE
⊢GNATS FROM DUST⊣
(EXODUS 8:16—19)

"Pray to your God to take away the frogs," Pharaoh said to Moses. "Then I will let your people go." Moses prayed, and God caused all the frogs to die. Only the frogs in the Nile River remained. Did Pharaoh keep his promises? No! He hardened his heart. "You can't go," he told Moses.

Then the Lord told Moses, "Tell Aaron to stretch out your staff and strike the dust on the ground. Then the dust throughout Egypt will become gnats." Aaron stretched out his hand with the staff and struck the dust of the ground. At once, biting gnats appeared. They flew onto people and animals.

Pharaoh's magicians tried to make dust become gnats, too. This time they couldn't do anything with their magic tricks. "This is the finger of God," they said to Pharaoh. Still, Pharaoh had a hard heart and would not let God's people go.

God told Moses:

Get up early in the morning. Stand before Pharaoh as he goes to the water. Say to him, "This is what the Lord says: Let my people go to worship Me. If you refuse to let them go, I will send swarms of flies on you and all your people. They will fill the houses and cover the ground. This time, though, I will treat you differently than I do My people. In the land of Goshen where the Hebrews live, there will be no swarms of flies. Then you will know that I am in this land. I will do this miracle tomorrow."

The next day, swarms of flies poured into Pharaoh's palace and into the houses of his officials. The flies ruined everything where the Egyptians lived. But there were no flies in the land of Goshen.

Pharaoh called for Moses to come to him. "Go, sacrifice to your God here in this land," he told Moses.

"No," Moses replied. "We must take a three-day journey into the desert."

"All right," said Pharaoh. "You may go, but don't go far away. Now pray that God will take away the flies."

Moses prayed, and the Lord took away the flies. Not one fly remained. But again Pharaoh hardened his heart and would not let the people go.

⊢How This Animal Tale Can Help You⊣

Pharaoh's magicians worshiped false gods. Satan used them to fool people. He helped the magicians in their work. Satan has great power, but he doesn't have all power. So he couldn't help the magicians make gnats from dust.

Satan and his demons still fool people today. How do they do it? One way is through witchcraft or fortune telling. "I'll tell you about your future," a fortuneteller may say. Or a person who calls herself a witch may promise, "I'll help you make right decisions." Satan and his demons control people like that.

Do you want advice from Satan or God? You can be sure of right advice if you read the Bible and pray to God. He is the only One who knows your future.

⊢MAZE:
WHERE SHOULD YOU GO FOR HELP?⊣

The circles across the top connected with the puzzle enclose several ways by which people try to find answers to life's problems. Some are connected with God, and some are connected with Satan. Trace pencil lines through the maze from each circle to its source at the bottom. Color red the lines that lead to God. Color green the lines that lead to Satan.

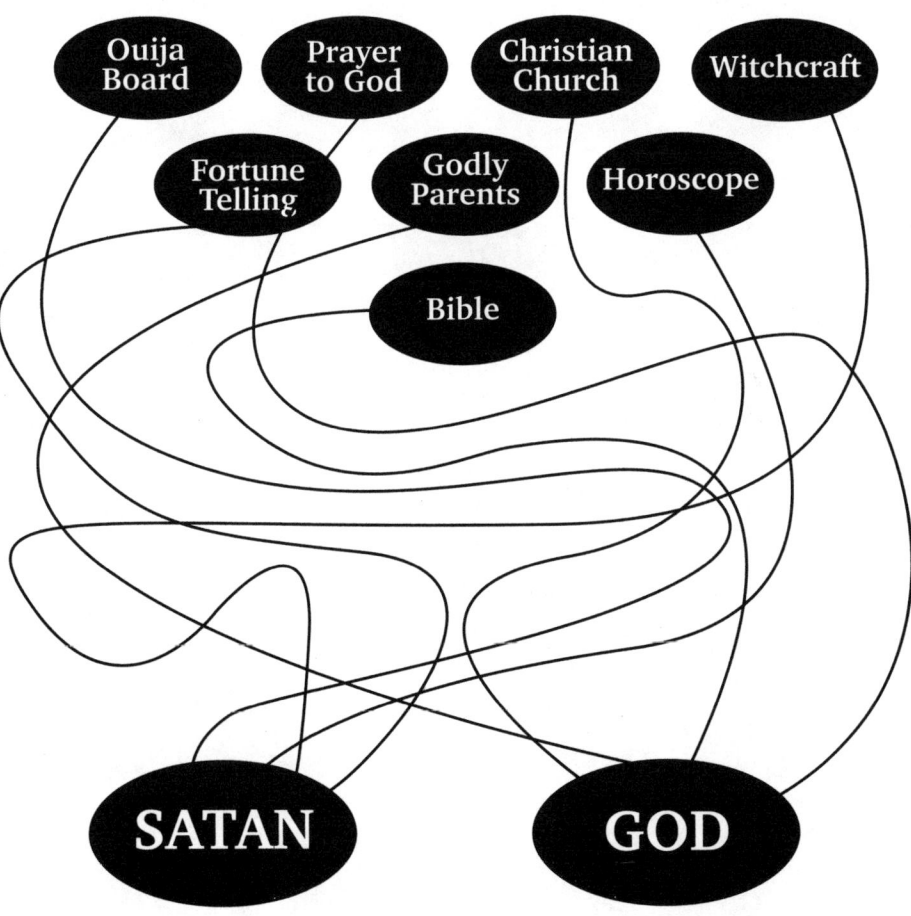

12
Plagues 5 and 6 on Egypt: Diseased Animals & Boils

"'The hand of the Lord will bring a terrible plague on your livestock in the field—on your horses and donkeys and camels and on your cattle and sheep and goats.' Festering boils broke out on men and animals."

—Exodus 9:3, 10

A man opened an envelope that had come in the mail. It contained a white powder. Soon the man got sick and died. Other people received similar envelopes. Scientists examined the white powder and discovered it was anthrax. Newspapers and television news programs warned the public to be careful when opening mail.

Anthrax is a severe contagious disease of warm-blooded animals and man. It isn't always fatal to people, but they can be very sick. The animals have chills, fever, and convulsions. Most of them die very suddenly. In the fifth plague, God caused the livestock in Egypt to get a terrible disease and die.

ANIMAL FACTS
⊢DISEASES AND BOILS
ON THE EGYPTIAN LIVESTOCK⊣

What was the disease the animals got? This disease was possibly anthrax.

Did it make much difference to the Egyptians if they lost their livestock? This plague must have been very hard on the Egyptians. They used oxen for laboring in the fields. They rode donkeys, camels, and horses as their chief means of transportation. Bulls were objects of worship.

What were the boils like? A boil, a hard round infection of the skin, contains a lot of pus and pressure on the nerves. Boils cause much suffering.

BIBLE ANIMAL TALE
⊢ DEAD ANIMALS
ALL OVER THE FIELDS⊢
(EXODUS 9:1⊢12)

"Go to Pharaoh again," God told Moses. "Tell him he must let my people go, so they can worship Me. If he won't let them go, the hand of the Lord will bring a terrible disease on the livestock in the fields. The horses, donkeys, camels, cattle, sheep, and goats will get this disease. Also tell Pharaoh that no animal belonging to the Israelites will die. I will do this thing tomorrow in the land."

Pharaoh didn't care what God said, and he didn't change his ways. So God sent the bad disease, and many Egyptian animals died. This time Pharaoh sent men to see what had happened to the animals of the Hebrews. Not one had died.

Their animals were very important to the Egyptians. Did Pharaoh change after the animals died? No. He still said, "No! No! No! You can't go!"

Next God told Moses, "Take handfuls of soot from a furnace and toss it into the air in the presence of Pharaoh. It will become fine dust over the whole land of Egypt. Festering boils will break out on people and on animals."

Moses stood in front of Pharaoh. He tossed the soot into the air. Just as God had said, boils broke out on people and on animals. The magicians couldn't even try to do that. They couldn't stand up because of the boils all over their bodies!

After these six awful plagues, did Pharaoh let God's people go? No, indeed. He was as stubborn as ever.

⊢How This Animal Tale Can Help You⊣

By these fifth and sixth plagues, God showed Pharaoh two things:

1. God has more power than people have. (Pharaoh's magicians could not do what God did.)

2. God treats His people differently from the way He treats those that hate Him. (The terrible disease and the boils did not bother the Israelites.)

God loves all people. In many ways, He treats us all the same. He gives us fresh air to breathe. He keeps the sun shining and sends us rain. He also allows storms and troubles to come on all people sometimes.

What is the difference, then? One big difference is that God promises to answer the prayers of His children. We can pray to Him when troubles come, and He will do what is best for us. People who don't belong to Him can't count on having prayers answered.

Here's another big difference: The Bible says that all things work together for good to those that love God. Remember that when trouble comes. Then God will give you peace and joy as you wait for Him to bring good out of your trouble.

⊢CODED MESSAGE:
WHAT IS GOD LIKE?⊣

Does God really know what's best for you? Will He always treat you right? Will God always be alive to help you? Does He have the power to take care of you? Read the verses below and use the code to find the answers.

a = ★	e = ♥	i = ☻	o = ☾

1. God l__v__s f__r__v__r. Psalm 135:13
   ☻   ♥   ☾   ♥   ♥

2. God kn__ws __v__ryth__ng. Psalm 44:21
   ☾   ♥ ♥   ☻

3. God s__ __s __ll th__gs. Proverbs 15:3
   ♥   ♥   ★   ☻

4. God can d__ __nyth__ng He wants to do. Jeremiah 32:17
   ☾   ♥   ☻

5. God is l__v__. 1 John 4:8
   ☾   ♥

6. God never ch__ng__s. Malachi 3:6
   ★   ♥

7. God is always f__ __r and r__ght. Revelation 15:3
   ★   ☻   ☻

Since all of these things are true about God, and if Jesus is your Savior, can you count on Him to do what is best for you at all times?   ○ Yes   ○ No

13
PLAGUES 7 AND 8 ON EGYPT: HAIL & LOCUSTS

"Throughout Egypt hail struck everything in the fields—both men and animals. By morning the wind had brought the locusts; they settled down in every area of the country in great numbers. "
—Exodus 9:25; 10:13-14

Has this ever happened to you? You come in from school and call out, "Hey, Mom, what's there to eat? I'm going to starve if I don't get some food right away!"

"I'm about out of groceries," your mom says, "but there are some vegetables in the refrigerator." "Vegetables? Yuck! May I go and buy a hamburger?" you ask.

If your mom didn't let you buy the hamburger, would you truly have starved? No. A person who is really starving would have gladly eaten the vegetables. Moses warned Pharaoh that he must obey God. If not, God would send plagues to destroy the crops. This could mean a famine in Egypt. Did Pharaoh then obey God? Find out in this devotion about the plagues of hail and locusts.

ANIMAL FACTS
⊢HAILSTONES HIT THE ANIMALS AND A LOCUST INVASION⊣

⊢HAIL⊣

What causes hail to fall? Hailstones are lumps of ice that fall from the sky. They can be as small as peas or as large as golf balls or even baseballs. Hail usually occurs in warm weather. The air near the earth is very warm, but it's freezing high above the earth. In a thunderstorm, strong wind currents move up and down between the cold and warm air. Ice crystals form and become layers of clear ice and compact snow, forming lumps or balls.

⊢LOCUSTS⊣

What are locusts? They are in the same family as grasshoppers. They travel together in huge swarms that can appear like a giant black cloud. There can be millions of them, so closely packed that they seem to blot out the sun. When they arrive at a good spot to get food, they swoop down together. Then they will eat every bit of vegetation in sight.

BIBLE ANIMAL TALE
⊢HAILSTONES KILL ANIMALS; LOCUSTS EAT THEIR FOOD⊣
(EXODUS 9:13–35; 10:1–20)

Moses stood before Pharaoh again and said, "God says, 'I could have already destroyed you, but I didn't so that I could show you My power. But you still defy Me and won't let My people go. At this time tomorrow I will send the worst hailstorm Egypt has ever seen. Order your people to bring in their slaves and their animals to a place of shelter. The ones left in the fields will die.'"

Some Egyptians feared the word of the Lord. They brought in their slaves and their livestock. Others took a chance and left them in the fields.

At God's command, Moses stretched out his staff toward the sky. Lightning flashed, thunder boomed, and hailstones fell. No such storm had ever come on Egypt before. Hailstones struck men and animals in the fields. They beat down everything in the fields and stripped every tree. Only the land of Goshen, where the Hebrews lived, was spared.

Pharaoh begged Moses, "Pray to the Lord. We've had enough thunder and hail. I will let you go." Moses left the city. He prayed and the storm stopped. Did Pharaoh keep his promise then? No. His old heart was still hard, and he would not let Israel go.

Again, Moses asked Pharaoh to let the people go. Again he refused. "God will send locusts into your land tomorrow," Moses warned him. "They will cover the ground. They will devour the little bit you have left after the hail. They will fill your houses—something you have never seen before." Then Moses walked away.

This worried Pharaoh's officials. They pleaded with Pharaoh, "Let the people go. Don't you know Egypt is ruined?"

Pharaoh called for Moses and Aaron to come back. He told them, "Go, worship the Lord your God. But who will be going?" When Moses said that all the people and their animals would go, Pharaoh said, "No! Have only the men go."

At God's command, Moses stretched out his staff over Egypt. God made an east wind blow all day and night. By morning, the wind had brought a huge army of locusts.

The locusts swarmed over everything. They ate all that the hail had left. Nothing green on trees and plants remained. Only the land of the Hebrews had no locusts.

Pharaoh called for Moses. "Ask your God to take away the locusts," he pleaded. The Lord changed the wind to a very strong west wind that blew all the locusts into the Red Sea. Did Pharaoh let the Hebrews go then? No. He was the same old hardhearted man.

⊢HOW THIS ANIMAL TALE
CAN HELP YOU⊣

Pharaoh tried to get his way by bargaining with Moses three times:

"I'll let you quit work for three days to worship your God here in Egypt."

"You may go, but take only the men."

In the ninth plague, he said, "All the people may go, but leave the animals here."

Pharaoh knew that if the Hebrews left their families or animals behind, they would return to Egypt. We can't obey God halfway. That didn't work for Pharaoh, and it won't work for us. Pharaoh had heart trouble—not his physical heart, but the place of his inner self that thinks, feels, and decides. He had a hard heart that would not yield to God. That's why he would not obey God.

How about your heart? Is it hard or tender toward God? If you have a tender heart, you will love God with your whole being. Then you you'll want to obey Him completely.

⊢TOTAL ALL ⊢OUT
LOVE FOR GOD⊣

God wants our total loyalty—not a halfway love and obedience. This means our hearts must be right. Solve the puzzle to learn how to get that kind of heart. Write in the blanks in #1 below by using every other letter, beginning with the first one, inside the heart. Then fill in the blanks in #2 by using all the remaining letters. Cross out each letter as you use it.

1. Man looks at the outward _ _ _ _ _ _ _ _ _ _ _ _, but the Lord looks at the _ _ _ _ _ _. He knows the _ _ _ _ _ _ _ _ of the heart. He says that a sinner's heart is _ _ _ _ _ _ _ _ _ and wicked. But if we will

_ _ _ _ _ _ _ _ _ in our heart and _ _ _ _ _ _ _ _ _ with our mouth the Lord Jesus, we will be _ _ _ _ _ _.

2. After we are saved, _ _ _ _ _ _ wants us to _ _ _ _ _ Him with _ _ _ _ our _ _ _ _ _ _ _, _ _ _ _ our _ _ _ _ _, and _ _ _ _ our _ _ _ _ _. He said that we must store up

_ _ _ _ _ _ _ _ _ in _ _ _ _ _ _ _, for where our treasure is, there our _ _ _ _ _ _ will be also.

```
A J P E P S E U A S R L A O N V
C E E A H L E L A H R E T A S R
E T C A R L E L T S S O D U E L
C A E L I L T M F I U N L D B T
  E R L E I A E S V U E R C
  E O H N E F A E V S E
    S N S H A E V A
      E R D T
```

14
PLAGUES 9 AND 10 ON EGYPT:
DARKNESS & DEATH OF THE FIRSTBORN

"Moses stretched out his hand toward the sky, and total darkness covered all Egypt for three days. 'Every firstborn son in Egypt will die... and the firstborn of the cattle as well.'"

—Exodus 10:22; 11:5

"But you promised!" Have you ever said that to your parents? Maybe they promised to take you to the beach on a certain day. The day arrives, but you don't go to the beach. Your dad's boss ordered him to work, or your mom didn't feel well. You are very disappointed, and you feel let down. Your parents are sorry, but something happened they couldn't control.

When God makes a promise that something will happen, it truly will happen. You can count on it. He never breaks His promises, because He knows ahead of time exactly what He will do.

Sometimes God's promises come with a condition. That is, He will keep His promise to us if we will do something first. It's like this: your parents promise to take you to the beach if you do all your homework first. No homework—no trip. If you don't do your homework, they won't break their promise when they don't take you to the beach.

ANIMAL FACTS
⊢CATTLE & EGYPTIAN ANIMAL GODS⊣

⊢CATTLE⊣

What are cattle? In the Bible the word cattle usually refers to livestock, like sheep, cows, donkeys, and horses.

⊢EGYPTIAN ANIMAL GODS⊣

What were the Egyptian gods? The Egyptians worshipped false gods—not the true God. They thought these gods controlled the rain and the growth of crops and were in charge of birth and death. Many of their nature gods were represented by animals, such as a bull, ram, falcon, crocodile, jackal, etc. One god was a part-human and part-animal statue.

BIBLE ANIMAL TALE
⊢BLACK DARKNESS & LAMB'S BLOOD ON THE DOORFRAMES⊣
EXODUS 10:21–29; 11:1–10; 12:21–29

"Stretch out your hand toward the sky," God told Moses. "Darkness will spread over Egypt—darkness that can be felt." Moses did that, and total darkness covered all Egypt for three days, except where the Hebrews lived. The Egyptians groped around in the blackness. They couldn't even see each other close by. No one dared to go outside for three days.

Not many of the Egyptians' animals had survived the terrible plagues. The ones that were left must have been very hungry and frightened. But no one came to take care of them. The Hebrews' animals were okay.

Pharaoh called for Moses to come. "Go, worship the Lord. Even your women and children may go," he said. "Only leave your flocks and herds here."

"No," replied Moses. "We will need animals for our sacrifices and burnt offerings to give to God. We won't know which ones until we get there."

"Get out!" yelled Pharaoh. "Don't come before me again."

"Just as you say," said Moses. "But the Lord told me He will send one more plague. After that, you will let us go. Tonight, about midnight, God will go throughout Egypt. Every firstborn son in Egypt will die. Your son will die. Your servants' sons will die. Even the firstborn of your cattle will die. But among the Hebrews, all will be quiet. Not a dog will bark at any man or animal."

Before this, Moses had called all the leaders of the Hebrews together. He told them, "God says we must count this month as the first month of our year. Today is the first day. On the fourteenth day, each family must kill a lamb at twilight. Then take a bunch of hyssop (a kind of shrub) and dip it in the animal's blood. Put some of the blood on the top and on both sides of the doorframe of your house.

"The Lord will go through the land to strike down the Egyptians. He will see the blood on the doorframes of your houses and will pass over them. He won't permit the death angel to enter your houses and strike you down."

At midnight of the 14th day the Lord killed all the firstborn sons in Egypt. From Pharaoh's son to the son of the prisoner in the dungeon, all firstborn sons died. Even the firstborn of all the livestock died. Pharaoh, all his officials, and all the other Egyptians wailed loudly, for someone was dead in every house. What happened to the firstborn sons of the Hebrews? Find out in the next devotion.

⊢How This Animal Tale Can Help You⊣

Pharaoh didn't believe God would do what He said. Even after many plagues, he still stubbornly refused to obey God. Then, in the tenth plague, his son died.

After that, he let the Hebrews go. Egypt was totally ruined. It never did rise to the height of power and glory it had before the plagues.

Pharaoh disobeyed God and lost everything. God promised He would send terrible trouble if he disobeyed. After ten plagues, Pharaoh finally understood that God keeps His promises.

God's promises can be good or bad for us. Here is a promise: "And this is what he promised us—even eternal life" (1 John 2:25). Who can claim that promise? "Whoever believes in the Son has eternal life, but whoever rejects the Son will not see life, for God's wrath remains on him" (John 3:36).

If we believe in Jesus as Savior, God gives us eternal life. That's good! If we reject Jesus, we are under God's wrath. That's bad! Either way, God always keeps His promises.

⊢GOD KEEPS HIS GREATEST PROMISE⊣

Long before He created the world, God planned to make and keep a certain promise to people. What was it? When did He keep it? Fill the blanks in the answer with the letters below using the geometrical descriptions for each number.

1. In the triangle and circle, but not in the cross.
2. In the cross, circle, and triangle.
3. In the circle only, but not in the cross or triangle.
4. In the cross and circle, but not in the triangle.
5. In the cross only, but not in the circle or triangle.
6. In the cross and triangle, but not in the circle.
7. In the triangle, but not in the circle or cross.

What was the promise?

Answer: God promised to send a Savior, so that whoever believed in Him might go to heaven.

When did He keep the promise?

God kept His promise when Jesus died for $\underline{\hspace{0.5cm}}$ $\underline{\hspace{0.5cm}}$ $\underline{\hspace{0.5cm}}$
$\qquad\qquad\qquad\qquad\qquad\qquad\qquad\qquad\quad$ 1 $\qquad$ 2 $\qquad$ 3

$\underline{\hspace{0.5cm}}$ $\underline{\hspace{0.5cm}}$ $\underline{\hspace{0.5cm}}$ $\underline{\hspace{0.5cm}}$.
4 $\qquad$ 5 $\qquad$ 6 $\qquad$ 7

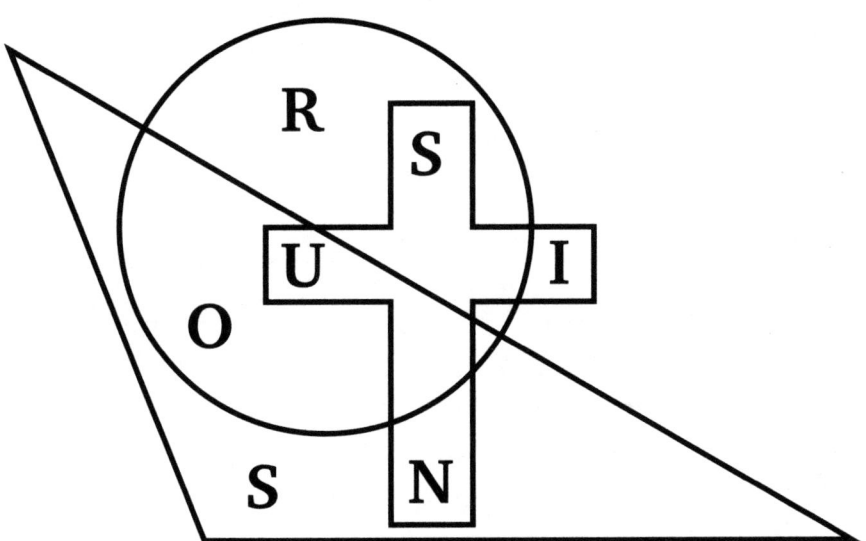

15

PERFECT LITTLE LAMBS OR KIDS

*"The animals you choose must be year-old males without defect, and you may take them from the sheep or the goats."
—Exodus 12:5*

What is your favorite holiday? The two most favorite Christian holidays are Christmas and Easter. They celebrate Jesus' birth and resurrection.

Just before they left Egypt, the Hebrews celebrated their first Passover Feast. Can you think why they called it "Passover"? (Hint: What did God do at the houses where blood was on the doorframes? He _____ _____ them.) God told His people to celebrate this feast each year, and He told them how to celebrate it. Everything about the celebration had a special meaning. The most important part of the celebration was eating a roasted lamb or kid.

ANIMAL FACTS
⊢LAMBS & KIDS⊣

⊢LAMBS⊣

What are lambs? Lambs are young sheep. All through Bible times, sheep were very important in the lives of the Hebrews. Do you remember that the second person born in the world was a shepherd?

⊢KIDS⊣

What are kids? We often call children "kids." Kid animals are young goats. The Hebrews valued goats. They wove goat's hair into a rough cloth. They drank goat's milk and also made cheese from it.

Did sheep and goats live together? Hebrew shepherds often owned goats as well as sheep. Many times the two animals grazed together in the fields. Goats are more independent and willful than the gentle sheep.

⊢SACRIFICIAL LAMBS OR KIDS⊣

Could the Hebrews choose sick or injured animals to sacrifice? No. God told His people they must sacrifice only perfect lambs or certain other animals. They must have no defects, like cuts or broken bones. This is because they represented Jesus, who would be the sacrifice for our sins. Jesus was absolutely perfect.

BIBLE ANIMAL TALE
⊢A ROASTED LAMB FOR THE TRAVELERS⊣
(EXODUS 12:1–30)

(In this story we will imagine we are watching a Hebrew family in Egypt.)

It was the fourteenth day of the first month. "This is a very special day," a Hebrew father told his children. "Four days ago, I chose a year-old lamb from our flock, as God said to do. I looked him over carefully. He has no defect. Tonight we will roast him for our supper.

"Now we must pack all our belongings and get dressed for a long trip," the father said. "We are going back to the land God promised He would give to Abraham and his descendants."

Can't you imagine the excitement of the children? They had never gone on a trip anywhere. Their parents had always been slaves. Was it really true that now Pharaoh would let them leave?

At twilight the children watched their father kill their lamb. He gathered a bunch of stems from a little bushy plant called hyssop and dipped it in the lamb's blood. Then he put the blood on the top and the two sides of their doorframe. "Are you sure you are doing this exactly right?" asked the firstborn son. "I don't want to die."

"You will be quite safe," the father assured him. "I have followed God's instructions."

The father roasted the lamb over a fire. He tended it carefully. The mother prepared the rest of the food for their feast. She made flat bread, with no leaven in it to make it rise. She also prepared some bitter herbs. When the supper was ready, they sat down to eat. They ate all of the lamb, as God had said to do.

Midnight came. "I'm alive!" exclaimed the firstborn son.

"Thank God!" said the father. "He protected you because of the blood."

All over the land, the Egyptian people wept loudly. In each house, the firstborn son was dead. Pharaoh called for Moses. "Get out of here!" Pharaoh bellowed. "All of you Hebrews leave. Take your flocks and herds with you. Worship the Lord as you asked to do. And bless me, too."

All the Hebrews marched away, as happy as could be. There were 600,000 men, besides women and children. Many other people who weren't Hebrews went with them, along with huge droves of flocks and herds. After 430 years in Egypt, they were free! And now they were going home.

How This Animal Tale Can Help You

The firstborn sons of the Hebrews were safe that special night. Why? They stayed inside a house where blood was on the doorframes. If they had walked outside, they would have died. Inside, the blood protected them. God loved His special people, and He made a way for them to escape death.

God loves all people, but He hates sin. How many people have sinned? "All have sinned and fall short of the glory of God" (Romans 3:23). Sinners are slaves to sin, just as the Hebrews were slaves in Egypt. God can't overlook our sin. He must punish sin. "The wages of sin is death" (Romans 6:23). God loves us, so He made a way of escape from the slavery of sin and death. Jesus died on the cross and shed His blood for our sins. Then He rose again.

The blood on the doorframes in Egypt reminds us of Jesus' blood. Jesus is the Door with bloodstains on it. When we believe in Him as Savior, we enter this Door, and we are saved. Have you entered this Door? If not, would you like to do it? *(See the last page of this book.)*

⊢MATCH⊢UP: THIS MEANS THAT⊢

Many things and events in this story have special meanings. God uses them as object lessons to help us understand the Bible. For instance, the bitter herbs in this story stand for the trials of slavery. Leaven in the Bible always stands for sin. The things and events are listed on the left side below. Can you figure out which meaning matches which thing or event? Draw a line between the two that you think match. Check your work in the "Answers" section in the back of the book. *(Continues on next page).*

THINGS AND EVENTS	THEIR MEANINGS
1. Slaves	A. Jesus is perfect
2. The lamb that was killed	B. Leaving the old life behind after salvation
3. No defects allowed on the lamb	C. God passed over the houses with blood on the doors
4. The Passover Feast	D. Sinners are servants of sin and Satan
5. The door with blood on it	E. The trials of slavery
6. The bitter herbs	F. Jesus, the Lamb of God
7. Leaven	G. Jesus, the Door of salvation
8. The slaves leaving Egypt	H. Sin

16
Horse-drawn Chariots & Fleeing Israelites

"The Egyptians—all Pharaoh's horses and chariots, horsemen and troops—pursued the Israelites and overtook them as they camped by the sea."
—Exodus 14:9

Has this ever happened to you? You are in some kind of trouble, and you don't think there's any way out. Then suddenly everything is O. K. *"Whew!"* you say. "I'm glad that mess is fixed up!" But WHAM! Another bad thing happens, and things are out of control again. What can you do?

Sometimes we can figure out for ourselves how to get out of trouble. But sometimes there is no way to escape. You can't help yourself, and no other human being can help you.

The Hebrews had just escaped the terrible trouble of slavery. Then they ran smack into more trouble. They thought they were trapped when Pharaoh and all his army, with horses and chariots, chased them.

ANIMAL FACTS
⊢HORSES⊢

More than 150 verses in the Bible refer to horses. Most Hebrews in their early days did not own horses. They rode donkeys and plowed with oxen. Later, some kings of Israel used many horses, especially in battles.

At least 4,000 years ago Indo-European nomads east of the Black Sea domesticated horses. The horse has been a faithful servant and friend of man for many years. Some horses are big and strong enough to pull heavy loads. Others are lightweight and fast. They can run in races.

BIBLE ANIMAL TALE
⊢EGYPTIANS & HORSES DROWN IN THE SEA⊣
(EXODUS 13:17-22; 14:1-31)

The happy Hebrews marched away from Pharaoh and the Egyptians. God led them. By day He went ahead of the people in a tall cloud to guide them. By night He showed them the way with a tall cloud of fire. Soon they set up camp at the Red Sea.

Back in his palace, Pharaoh paced the floor. "What have we done?" he asked his officials. "We let the Hebrews go, and now they are not here to serve us."

Pharaoh barked out orders to his men: "Get my chariot ready for travel. Gather together six hundred of the best chariots with all the other chariots of Egypt. Place officers over all of them. "Let's go!" Pharaoh ordered, and they started out after their former slaves.

As Pharaoh approached their camp, the Hebrews looked up. "The Egyptians are coming after us!" they cried. Terrified, they cried out to the Lord for help. They said to Moses, "Was it because there were no graves in Egypt that you brought us out here to die? We'd be better off serving the Egyptians than dying in the desert."

"Don't be afraid," Moses answered. "Stand firm and see the deliverance of the Lord. You will never see the Egyptians again. The Lord will fight for you. Just be still."

The Lord told Moses, "Raise your staff over the sea to divide the water. Then My people can go through the sea on dry ground."

The angel of God, who had been traveling in front of the Hebrews, went behind them. So did the tall cloud. It came between the armies of Egypt and the Hebrews. It brought light to God's people and darkness to the Egyptians.

Moses stretched out his hand over the sea. All night God caused a strong east wind to drive the sea back, until there was a path of dry land. The Hebrews walked through the sea on dry ground, with a wall of water on either side of them.

All Pharaoh's horses and chariots and horsemen followed hard after the Hebrews. They started into the sea to cross on dry land, too. But God caused the wheels of their chariots to fall off. The confused charioteers couldn't drive their chariots. "Let's get away from God's people!" they cried. "The Lord is fighting for them."

"Stretch out your hand over the sea," God told Moses. At daybreak, the waters started back into place. The Egyptians tried to escape, but the waters covered the chariots and horsemen. Pharaoh and his entire army drowned.

Miriam, the sister of Moses and Aaron, sang: "Sing to the Lord, for he is highly exalted. The horse and its rider he has hurled into the sea."

⊢HOW THIS ANIMAL TALE CAN HELP YOU⊣

When the Hebrews saw the Egyptians coming after them, they complained. How quickly they had forgotten what God had done! He showed them His great power in the ten plagues He sent on Egypt. He delivered His people from slavery. But now they thought they were doomed. Once again, God showed them He was in control when he drowned Pharaoh and his army in the sea.

When troubles come, do you forget that God is in control? He is in charge of everything. Sometimes He allows bad things to happen, and you won't always understand why. But you can know God will allow only what is in His plan for you.

God's plan is to work out all things for good. Moses told the Hebrews to be still and let God work. Sometimes we have to wait for God to help us. If we trust Him while we wait, we can know He will do what is best for us.

⊢CHOOSE THE WORDS: WHAT TO DO WHEN TROUBLE COMES⊣

Circle the word in each square that doesn't belong. Write those words, in order, on the first set of blanks. The sentence will be scrambled. Unscramble the words and write them on the second set of blanks to find a special verse for you when trouble comes.

GO COME WITH	UP LEAN DOWN	HEART BLUE GREEN	EYES EARS TRUST	FLOWERS LORD GRASS
EGSS BACON IN	UNDERSTANDING COMPUTER TYPEWRITER	WALK RUN THE	ALL BOY GIRL	TOE FINGER AND
CRY YOUR LAUGH	NOT BIG SMALL	ON BALL BAT	HORSE OWN COW	YOUR CITY TOWN

1. _____ _____ _____
_____ _____ _____
_____ _____ _____
_____ _____ _____
_____ _____ _____.

2. "_____ _____ _____
_____ _____ _____
_____ _____ _____
_____ _____ _____
_____ _____ _____."

—Proverbs 3:5

17
Bushels of Quails for the Grumblers

"He rained meat down on them like dust, flying birds like sand on the seashore. He made them come down inside their camp, all around their tents."
—Psalm 78:27-28

"Oh, no! Spinach again? I hate spinach," a boy complains. "Why can't I eat something else?"

A girl says, "Mom, I'm ready for my dessert." Her mother looks at her daughter's plate. Everything is gone but the carrots.

"You must eat your carrots before you get dessert," Mom says. "Aw, Mom, carrots are yucky," the girl fusses. "But I do want my dessert."

Do these conversations sound familiar to you? The Bible story in this devotion tells of people who complained about their food—not to their mothers, but to God. The story of the quails tells what God did.

ANIMAL FACTS
⊢QUAILS⊣

Do quails live in trees and make their nests in them? No. Quails are ground dwellers. They eat insects and scratch for their food on the ground.

Do quails fly well? Yes, they have strong flying muscles for rapid flight for short distances. When migrating, they stretch their wings and allow the wind to bear them along. At the end of a long flight, they arrive very exhausted.

Did quails live in the desert when the Hebrews passed through it? No. They came near it as they migrated northward from southern countries.

Are quails good for food? The birds are quite plump after wintering in the south, and they make good eating.

BIBLE ANIMAL TALE
⊢QUAIL MEAT BETWEEN THEIR TEETH⊣
(NUMBERS 11:4–34)

March, march, march! The Hebrews followed God's tall cloud from the Red Sea southeast into the desert. When the people didn't have enough food, God caused flakes that looked like frost to cover the ground in the mornings. They called it manna, meaning, "What is it?"

"It is bread the Lord has given you to eat," Moses told them. God provided manna for His people for forty years, until they came to their homeland.

As the people traveled, they camped at a place where there was no water. God told Moses to strike a big rock with his staff. When Moses struck the rock, cool, fresh water poured out from the rock.

Next, God led His people to camp near Mt. Sinai, where they stayed for a long time. There God gave them the Ten Commandments and other rules for living. Then they traveled on again, marching across the desert.

Some people began to complain. "If only we had meat to eat!" they grumbled. "In Egypt, we had plenty of food. We ate fish at no cost. We had cucumbers, melons, leeks, onions, and garlic. Now all we have is manna. We're tired of manna. We've lost our appetites."

Moses heard those complaints. The Lord heard them, too, and He became angry. He told Moses, "Tell the people they will eat meat tomorrow. I heard them when they wailed, 'If only we had meat to eat! We were better off in Egypt!'

"Tell them I will give them meat, and they will eat it—not just one day, or two days, or five, ten, or twenty days—but for a whole month, until it comes out of their noses. Why? Because they have grumbled about what I did for them."

God caused an east wind to blow from the sea that drove quails to the Hebrews' camp. They flew low over the camp, to about three feet above the ground. The people could just reach up and grab them.

All that day and night and all the next day, the people gathered quails. No one gathered less than about 60 bushels. They spread out the birds all around the camp. They cooked the birds and started to eat them. But when the meat was still between their teeth, God struck the complainers with a severe disease, and they died.

⊢How This Animal Tale Can Help You⊣

"My friends have new clothes. Why can't I have something new? I hate these old rags." Probably kids who say things like that really don't have rags. Their clothes are most likely still good, but they're just not the latest style.

Stop and think about all the good things God has done for you. He gives you food to eat, clothes to wear, and a place to live. Do you say that your parents provide all of these things for you? Who gives them the health, strength, and brains to hold down a job? God does. He has done so many things for all of us that we can never name them all.

When we grumble about what God gives us, He is not happy with us. We please Him when we are content and happy with what He does for us. Hebrews 13: 5 says, "Be content with what you have, because God has said, 'Never will I leave you; never will I forsake you.'" God is always with His children, and He promises to take care of our needs. Instead of grumbling, be grateful. "Let them give thanks to the Lord for his unfailing love and his wonderful deeds for men" (Psalm 107:8).

⊢THANK GOD FOR THESE THINGS⊣

Below is a list of a few of the many things God has given His children. You can probably think of many more. Try to fit the words from the list below in the blanks that include the letters of the word "thankfulness."

BIBLE   PARENTS   EARS   EYES
FOOD   CLOTHES   HOUSE   HEALTH
RAINFALL   FRIENDS   KINFOLKS   SUNSHINE

1. __ __ __ __ __ T __

2. __ __ __ __ __ H

3. __ A __ __ __ __ __ __

4. __ __ __ __ N __ __

5. K __ __ __ __ __ __ __

6. F __ __ __

7. __ __ U __ __

8. __ __ __ L __

9. __ __ N __ __ __ __ __

10. __ __ E __

11. __ __ __ S

12. __ __ __ __ __ __ S

18
POISONOUS SNAKES IN THE DESERT

"He led you through the vast and dreadful desert, that thirsty and waterless land, with its venomous snakes and scorpions."

–Deuteronomy 8:15

Do you hate to take bad-tasting medicine? If you mom offers you a spoonful, do you say, "Please don't make me take it! I'd rather be sick." You probably still have to take the medicine, because your mom knows you need it.

In this animal tale, the Hebrews got very sick; and some of them died. God provided a remedy for them, but it wasn't medicine to swallow. All they had to do was to look at a snake of bronze.

ANIMAL FACTS
⊶SNAKES⊷

Are there snakes in the desert where the Hebrews wandered? Yes. There are many types of snakes in the Sinai Peninsula.

Are there any poisonous kinds there? Yes, many kinds are poisonous. One deadly kind, the puff adder, is large and marked with yellow, flame-like markings. It puffs up and hisses loudly when it is disturbed. Some Bible versions call the snakes in this animal tale "fiery." Maybe it was the puff adder. Or it may have been a snake with a fiery bite.

BIBLE ANIMAL TALE
─SNAKEBITES & THE CURE─
(NUMBERS 21:1─9)

"Snakes! Snakes!" The cry rang out over all the camp of the Hebrews. Here was more trouble--and just when they were nearing their homeland! They had camped in the desert for forty years. All the people who had refused to go to Canaan had died. Then God let the new generation start out of the desert.

As they traveled, the Hebrews came to the lands of other people. When they tried to pass through Edom, its king with his army met them. "You can't pass through our land," the king said. Sadly, God's people turned back. They had to journey out of their way to go around Edom.

The people grew very impatient. "Why have you brought us up out of Egypt to die in the desert?" they said to Moses. "We have no bread!" *(Wrong! God had given them manna to eat for forty years.)* "Also, we have no water," the people said. *(Wrong again! God had supplied them with water, even bringing some out of a rock.)* "We detest this miserable food—this manna," they grumbled.

That's when the cry rang out, "Snakes! Snakes!" God caused a great invasion of poisonous snakes. They bit the people, and many died.

The people hurried to Moses. "We sinned when we spoke against the Lord and you," they said. "Pray to the Lord. Ask Him to take the snakes away!" So Moses prayed for them.

God said to Moses, "Make a snake and put it up on a pole. Any person who is bitten may look at the snake. Those who look will live." Moses made a bronze snake and set it up on a pole. To show what happened next, we will pretend to visit one family.

A little boy and his sister are playing outside their tent. Suddenly, a snake bites the boy. "Oh, a snake has bitten me!" he cries. "Run and tell Father."

The girl runs to the father and tells him the scary news about her brother. "Hurry and take him to look at the bronze snake," she begs. The father lifts the boy into his arms and rushes to stand before the bronze snake.

"Look at the snake," he urges his boy. "Believe that God will heal you." The little boy looks. At once the snakebite disappears, and he is well.

Then a snake bites an aunt in the family. Her son tries to take her to see the snake, but she refuses. "I am too sick. Don't move me," she says. "I don't think that looking at a bronze snake will heal me." Soon she dies.

HOW THIS ANIMAL TALE CAN HELP YOU

Even though the story about the one family is imaginary, it shows how the people may have acted. One thing we know for sure: the people who were bitten had two choices: (1) they could believe God and look at the snake or (2) they could refuse to look. Only the ones who believed God and looked stayed alive.

Jesus said, "Just as Moses lifted up the snake in the desert, so the Son of Man must be lifted up, that everyone who believes in him may have eternal life" (John 3:14-15). Jesus was talking about when He would be lifted up on the cross. There, He took our sins on Himself, and was punished for them. Thank God, He didn't stay dead. He came alive again on the third day.

We have two choices about Jesus' death and resurrection: (1) we can believe in Jesus or (2) we can refuse to believe in Him. Only those who believe in Jesus may have eternal life and live in heaven forever.

⊢WHO WAS LIFTED UP?⊣

Who was lifted up so that we might go to heaven by believing in Him? Color all the #1 squares red and the #2 squares yellow to find the answer.

2	2	2	2	2	2	2	2	2	2	2	2	2	2	2	2	2	2	2	2	2
2	2	2	1	2	1	1	1	2	1	1	1	2	1	2	2	1	2	1	1	1	2
2	2	2	1	2	1	2	2	2	1	2	2	2	1	2	2	1	2	1	2	2	2
2	2	2	1	2	1	1	2	2	1	1	1	2	1	2	2	1	2	1	1	1	2
2	2	2	1	2	1	2	2	2	2	2	1	2	1	2	2	1	2	2	2	1	2
2	1	1	1	2	1	1	1	2	1	1	1	2	1	1	1	1	2	1	1	1	2
2	2	2	2	2	2	2	2	2	2	2	2	2	2	2	2	2	2	2	2	2	2

19
A SCARED DONKEY SEES AN ANGEL

"When the donkey saw the angel of the Lord, standing in the road with a drawn sword in his hand, she turned off the road into a field."
—Numbers 22:23

Some schoolmates invited Jill to a party. She asked her dad if she might go. "I'm sorry," he said, "but I must say no. I have heard that some kids have drugs and alcohol at those parties."

Jill really wanted to go. Her schoolmates said, "Do like we do. Pretend to go to bed, and then slip out of the house when your dad is asleep."

That night Jill put on her party clothes and slipped into bed. She waited to hear her parents go to bed. But while she waited, a quiet voice seemed to say, "Don't go. Obey your parents. Obey your parents. Obey. . ." Jill got out of bed, put on her pajamas, and returned to bed. Soon she was sound asleep.

What was that voice? It was God, the Holy Spirit. He lived in Jill, who was a Christian. She obeyed Him and probably kept herself from some bad trouble.

When God spoke to a man in this animal tale, he used the voice of an angel, but He got his attention first with the voice of a donkey.

ANIMAL FACTS
⊢DONKEYS⊣

Were donkeys used in Bible times? Yes, donkeys are mentioned in more than 150 verses in the Bible.

Are donkeys stupid? No. A donkey can pick its way across rocky deserts where a man can hardly find a path. It needs only a bridle to guide it and can often find its own way.

Did only rich people own donkeys in Bible times? No. All classes of people owned them. Donkeys are economical to own. They eat only one-fourth as much fodder as a horse does.

BIBLE ANIMAL TALE
⊢A LITTLE TALK WITH A DONKEY⊣
(NUMBERS 22:1–41; 23:1–12)

A donkey clip-clopped down a path, ridden by a man named Balaam. This man, who practiced witchcraft, planned to go to the country of Moab. Why did he want to go to Moab? To find the answer we have to go back to the beginning of this story.

Balak, the king of Moab was terrified. The Hebrews, about three million of them, had camped in Moab by the Jordan River on their way to the promised land of Caanan, which lay on the other side of the river. "This horde of people will lick up everything around us, as an ox eats up grass," he said.

Balak sent messengers to Balaam. They told him, "Balak says,'Come at once and put a curse on these people who have moved in next to me. Maybe your curse will drive them away.'" Balaam replied, "Spend the night here. Then I will give you the answer God gives me." Somehow, Balaam knew about God. By his actions, though, he did not show that he believed in God.

During the night, God told Balaam, "Do not go with the messengers. You must not put a curse on those people, because I have blessed them."

The next morning, Balaam told the men, "Go back to your country. God will not give me permission to go with you."

Soon other, more important, men came and told Balaam, "Balak says, 'Don't let anything keep you from coming. I will pay you well. Come and put a curse on these people.'"

Again Balaam refused. God knew that Balaam really wanted to go and get money from Balak, so He said, "You may go, but you must bless My people; do not curse them." Balaam saddled his donkey and started on his way to Moab.

God was angry with Balaam for not wanting to obey Him in the first place. As the donkey walked, she suddenly saw an angel standing in their path! He had a sword in his hand. The donkey turned off the road into a field. Balaam beat the donkey and made her get back on the road.

Again the donkey saw the angel, standing before them on a narrow path between two walls. The donkey pressed close to the wall, crushing Balaam's foot. Balaam beat her again. Wham! Wham!

Next the angel stood in a narrow place where there was no room to turn. The donkey lay down under Balaam. Again Balaam beat her. This time the Lord opened the donkey's mouth. She said, "What have I done to you to make you beat me these three times?"

Balaam said to the donkey, "You have made a fool of me! If I had a sword, I'd kill you!"

"Did I ever do this to you before?" asked the donkey.

"No," admitted Balaam. Then God opened Balaam's eyes, and he saw the angel, holding the sword. Balaam fell face down in the path.

"Why did you beat your donkey?" asked the angel. "By now, I would have killed you, but she spared your life. Go on, but say only what God tells you to say."

Balak led Balaam to a high place overlooking the Hebrew camp. He waited for Balaam to curse God's people, but Balaam didn't do it. He blessed them three times. Balak was very angry. He struck his hands together and said, "You leave at once. I promised to pay you a big price, but now you will get nothing."

⊢HOW THIS ANIMAL TALE CAN HELP YOU⊣

God knew that Balaam didn't want to obey Him because he wanted the reward money. Finally, God let Balaam go, but He stopped him on his way. Then God used a donkey to talk to Balaam. After that, the angel told him what he must do. Balaam didn't get the reward money; and God didn't bless Him, either.

God knows whether we truly want to obey Him or not. When we think about disobeying, He speaks to us in a quiet voice inside. It is the voice of the Holy Spirit, urging us to do right. Pay attention! God blesses us when we obey Him. He may discipline us if we don't obey.

⊢WHEN WE DON'T OBEY⊣

In the puzzle, two Christian children are walking on the path of obeying God. The two others are Christians who have sinned. Trace a path for them to get back on the path of obedience by drawing lines between the words of this verse: "IF WE CONFESS OUR SINS, HE IS FAITHFUL AND JUST AND WILL FORGIVE US OUR SINS." —1 John 1:9

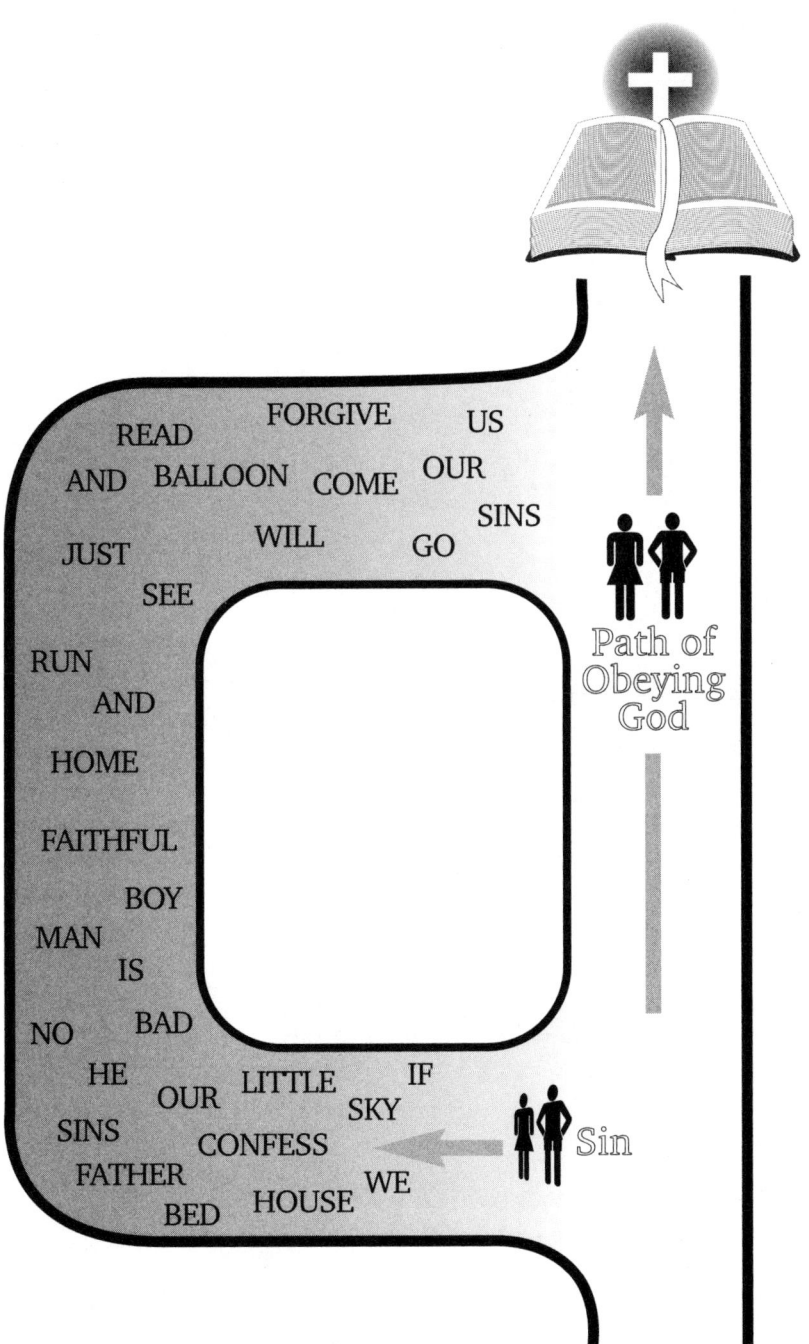

20
MULTITUDES OF CHARIOTS & HORSES

"They came out with all their troops and a large number of horses and chariots—a huge army, as numerous as the sand on the seashore."
—Joshua 11: 4

Do you have a lucky charm--a penny, a piece of jewelry, or some other item? A lucky charm is supposed to bring you good fortune and keep trouble away. A person who trusts in a lucky charm tries to carry it always.

A person who depends on a charm or other item for good fortune is not depending on God. He wants us to depend on Him--not on things or other persons. In this Bible animal tale, Joshua learned that God didn't want him to depend on chariot horses for winning his battles.

ANIMAL FACTS
⊢CHARIOT HORSES⊣

Were chariots used in battles? Yes. A warrior in a chariot pulled by fast horses could accurately shoot his bow or throw a spear. His opponent on a horse might find it hard to fight while riding.

How many horses pulled a chariot? Either two or four horses pulled the chariots. In a battle there were usually two charioteers—one to drive the chariot, and one to fire the bow.

Did the Hebrews own horses? Before the Hebrews entered Canaan, God told them, "The king, moreover, must not acquire great numbers of horses for himself " (Deuteronomy 17:16). God told Joshua to hamstring the horses he captured. *(To hamstring a horse is to make a small cut in the tendon of his leg. The horse can still walk afterwards, but he cannot run and fight in a battle any more.)*

BIBLE ANIMAL TALE
⊢HAMSTRING THE CHARIOT HORSES⊣
(JOSUA 10–11)

Home at last! At least, the Hebrews were almost there. They camped across the Jordan River from Jericho with all their belongings and animals. Moses had just died, and God named Joshua to lead His people.

Many fierce, warlike people lived in Canaan. They were very wicked and worshiped idols. "You must drive them out and possess the land," God told the Hebrews. "I gave this land long ago to Abraham and his descendants. These wicked people have moved into your land, and they will fight to keep it."

"Be strong and very courageous," God told Joshua. "Do not turn from My law, that you may be successful. Do not be terrified or discouraged, for the Lord your God will be with you."

Joshua led the Hebrews to the Jordan River. God stopped the water from flowing, and they walked across on dry ground. Then Joshua and his army had to conquer the city of Jericho. They followed God's directions and marched around the walls on six days. On the seventh day, they marched around seven times. They blew their trumpets and shouted a great shout. And then. . .

God sent the walls tumbling down! Joshua and his army walked in and destroyed with the sword every living thing— people, cattle, sheep, and donkeys.

Joshua and his army won victory after victory. In one battle, they needed more time. "Sun, stand still," Joshua commanded. God caused the sun to stand still for about a day, and the moon stopped moving across the sky. There was never another day like it. Joshua's army defeated their enemies. Some of them ran down a road to get away. God hurled large hailstones on them, and they died.

Joshua and his army took the whole south of the country. The kings of the north then got up a huge army. They came against the Hebrew army with a multitude of horses and chariots, as numerous as sand on the seashore.

The Lord said to Joshua, "Don't fear them. By this time tomorrow I will hand them over to you, dead. You must hamstring their horses and burn their chariots."

Joshua and his army sneaked up on their enemies. The Lord gave them a great victory. They defeated the wicked kings' armies and pursued them until no survivors were left. Then, as God had told him to do, Joshua hamstrung their horses and burned their chariots.

⊢HOW THIS ANIMAL TALE CAN HELP YOU⊣

Christians have a crafty, evil enemy, Satan. He hates God, and he also hates us. He wants us to disobey God and to sin. He attacks us with many temptations to do wrong. Whether we like it or not, we are in a warfare against Satan.

Are we as strong and wise as Satan? No. If we try to fight Satan all by ourselves, we'll lose the battle. Also, we can't depend on other people to fight our battles. Godly people can give us advice and pray for us, but they can't fight Satan for us.

God wants His people to depend on Him, not on horses and chariots to win battles. He doesn't want us to depend on lucky charms, other people, or ourselves. Depend on God for help. "Blessed are all who take refuge in him" (Psalm 2:12).

⊢WHERE DO YOU PLACE YOUR TRUST?⊣

Use the code to fill the blanks below. You will write a verse to help you in your fight with Satan.

A=1 E=5 I=9 O=13 U=17	B=2 F=6 L=10 R=14 W=18	C=3 G=7 M=11 S=15	D=4 H=8 N=12 T=16

"
___ ___ ___ ___   ___ ___ ___ ___ ___   ___ ___
15 13 11 5   16 14 17 15 16   9   12

___ ___ ___ ___ ___ ___ ___ ___   ___ ___ ___
3   8   1   14 9   13 16 15   1   12 4

___ ___ ___ ___   ___ ___
15 13 11 5   9   12

___ ___ ___ ___ ___ ___ ,   ___ ___ ___   ___ ___
8   13 14 15 5   15   2   17 16   18 5

___ ___ ___ ___ ___   ___ ___   ___ ___ ___
16 14 17 15 16   9   12   16 8   5

___ ___ ___ ___   ___ ___   ___ ___ ___
12 1   11 5   13 6   16 8   5

___ ___ ___ ___   ___ ___ ___   ___ ___ ___ ."
10 13 14 4   13 17 14   7   13 4

—Psalm 20:7

21

GIDEON FIGHTS AN ARMY
OF CAMEL RIDERS

"They came up with their livestock and their tents like swarms of locusts. It was impossible to count the men and their camels; they invaded the land to ravish it."
—Judges 6:5

When little boys pretend they are soldiers, they may use toy guns. To win battles in today's warfare, soldiers must have powerful weapons.

In ancient times the goal always was to have better weapons than the enemy had. When the Hebrews conquered their enemies in Canaan, their warriors had spears, javelins, and swords. In this Bible story, though, Gideon and his men had very strange weapons for fighting a huge army of camel riders.

ANIMAL FACTS
⊣CAMELS & LAPPING DOGS⊢

Why did the Midianites, enemies of the Hebrews, have many camels? The Midianites lived in the desert east and southeast of Canaan. Their warriors used camels for crossing the desert into Canaan.

Why did God tell Gideon to use only soldiers who lapped water with their tongues like a dog? These soldiers took water from the river with their hands and lapped it like a dog. If an enemy approached, they could keep their heads erect to see them and could quickly grab their weapons to fight. The men who knelt to drink from the river weren't alert.

BIBLE ANIMAL TALE
⊢A STRANGE BATTLE AGAINST AN ARMY OF CAMEL RIDERS⊣
(JUDGES 6–7)

The Hebrews began to disobey God and worship idols. So God let a huge army of Midianites invade their land for seven years. These nomads and their camels were so many they could not be counted. The Midianites camped on the land and ruined the crops. They didn't spare any living thing, not even sheep, cows, or donkeys.

"Help us," the Israelites begged God. One day God appeared to Gideon in the form of an angel. God told him, "I am sending you to save My people from the Midianites."

"How can I save Israel?" Gideon asked. "My family isn't strong, and I am the least in my family."

"I will be with you, and you will strike down all the Midianites together," the Lord answered.

The Midianites joined forces with other enemies of the Hebrews. They came and camped in a valley like swarms of locusts, with countless numbers of camels. Gideon blew a trumpet to call the Hebrew soldiers together. Thirty-two thousand men came. They camped to the south of their enemy's camp.

"You have too many men," God told Gideon. "Your soldiers will brag that they won in their own strength. Announce that anyone who is afraid may return home." Gideon made the announcement, and 22,000 men left.

"There are still too many soldiers," God said. "Take them to the river to drink. Notice the ones who lap the water with their tongues like a dog. Separate them from those who kneel to drink."

When the men drank, God told Gideon to send home the ones who knelt down. Only 300 men were left to fight the Midianites.

This little band of brave men camped on a hill above the Midianites. That night Gideon woke up his men. "Get up!" he said. "The Lord has given the Midianites into your hands."

Gideon divided the army into three companies. He gave each man a trumpet and an empty jar with a torch inside. "Do what I do," Gideon told his men.

Gideon and his hundred men crept up to the edge of the Midianites' camp. They blew their trumpets and broke the jars in their hands. The lights from their torches shone brightly. The other 200 soldiers did the same thing. Then they all shouted, "A sword for the Lord and for Gideon!"

The startled Midianites awoke. They heard the noise and saw the bright lights. They ran away fast, with Gideon and his men chasing them. God caused the frightened enemies to kill each other with their swords. Gideon and his men won a great victory. Was it by their own strength and mighty weapons? No, it was by God's miraculous power.

⊷How This Animal Tale Can Help You⊷

Satan is a Christian's enemy. God gives us a powerful sword— the Bible—to use in fighting him. When Satan tempted Jesus three times, Jesus used this sword. He quoted verses from the Bible, and Satan went away.

"Take the helmet of salvation and the sword of the Spirit, which is the word of God" (Ephesians 6:17). Read the Bible daily. Memorize verses that help you say no to Satan's temptations. When he tempts you, use your sword. Quote a Bible verse or remind yourself that the Bible says we should not sin. This will help you resist Satan's temptations.

⊷Use Your Sword⊷

You don't need to quote long Bible verses to use your sword of the Spirit against Satan. Often four or five words from a verse will help you. Some examples are given below. Use the code to fill the blanks. (For instance, 2W=C.)

	S	W	O	R	D
1	D	I	M	P	L
2	A	C	V	H	S
3	E	Y	O	R	N
4	B	T	U		

1. "_____ _____ _____ _____ _____ _____ _____ _____ , _____ _____ _____ _____
   2W 2R 1W 1D 1S 3R 3S 3D   3O 4S 3S 3W

_____ _____ _____ _____ _____ _____ _____ _____ _____ _____ _____."
3W 3O 4O 3R   1R 2S 3R 3S 3D 4W 2D

—Ephesians 6:1

2. "_____ _____ _____ _____ _____ _____ _____ _____ _____ _____
    1S   3O   3D   3O   4W   1D   1W   3S   4W   3O

_____ _____ _____ _____ _____ _____ _____ _____ _____."
 3S   2S   2W   2R   3O   4W   2R   3S   3R

—Colossians 3:9

3. "_____ _____ _____ _____ _____ _____ _____ _____ _____ _____ _____
    3W   3O   4O   2D   2R   2S   1D   1D   3D   3O   4W

_____ _____ _____ _____ _____."
 2D   4W   3S   2S   1D

—Exodus 20:15

4. "_____ _____ _____ _____ _____ _____ _____ _____ _____ _____ _____
    3W   3O   4O   2L   2R   2S   1D   1D   3D   3O   4W

_____ _____ _____ _____ _____."
 2W   3O   2O   3S   4W

—Exodus 20:17

5. "_____ _____ _____ _____ _____ _____ _____ _____
    1D   3O   2O   3S   3W   3O   4O   3R

_____ _____ _____ _____ _____ _____ _____."
 3S   3D   3S   1O   1W   3S   2D

—Matthew 5:44

22
MOTHER COWS, GOLDEN RATS & A FISH GOD

"They took two such cows and hitched them to the cart and penned up their calves."

—1 Samuel 6:10, 11

"I really need God to help me in my final exams," says a girl. "I'll wear my chain with the gold cross. Then He will help me."

"I want our basketball team to win the pennant this year," says a boy. "I'm going to pray and ask God to help us do it. I haven't prayed much before. I hope I'll do it right."

Do you think either the boy or the girl will have God's help? We can't sway God to help us by doing religious acts when our hearts aren't right. The Israelites found that out when they took the Ark of God to their battlefield.

ANIMAL FACTS
⊷COWS, RATS & A FISH GOD⊶

⊷COWS⊶

Were cows used as work animals in early days? Yes. They were raised for their milk and meat, but they were also work animals. They pulled plows and other farm equipment. The cows in this story had never pulled a cart or wagon before.

Why did the two cows in this story "moo" as they walked? The cows both had young calves. A mother cow takes care of her young calf and gives it milk until it is old enough to eat grass and grains. She wouldn't like to leave her calf alone for long. That's why these cows "mooed" while walking away.

⊷RATS⊶

How were rats destructive in Bible days? Swarms of them devastated grain crops. They also gave people serious diseases.

⊷A FISH GOD⊶

Who worshiped a fish god? One enemy of the Hebrews, the Philistines, worshiped an idol named Dagon. It had a head, shoulders, arms, and upper part of a man. The lower part was in the form of a fish.

BIBLE ANIMAL TALE
⊢MOOING COWS PULL A STRANGE LOAD⊣
(1 SAMUEL 4–6)

Two cows, pulling a cart, walked into the land of the Hebrews. The Ark of God was on the cart, along with a chest. The chest contained five gold models of rats and five gold models of tumors. The Ark should have been in the tabernacle. How did it get on the cart? Why were the items in the chest with it? This is how it happened:

"Drive out all the wicked people in the land I gave you," God had told the Hebrews. They didn't do this completely. One enemy, the Philistines, settled on the coast and caused much trouble. One day the Hebrews fought the Philistines and lost the battle, with 400 of their men killed.

"We need God's help," the Hebrews said. "Let's bring the Ark of God to our battlefield." When the Ark arrived, the people shouted with excitement. Instead of winning the battle, though, they lost in a big way. The Philistines killed 30,000 foot soldiers and captured the Ark. They took it to their home and put it in the temple of Dagon, an idol they worshipped.

The next day the Philistines saw the statue of Dagon fallen on its face before the ark. They put it back up again. The next morning they found the statue fallen again, with its head and hands broken off. It was lying in the doorway.

The people in that city got sick with a terrible plague that caused painful tumors. Also, rats devastated their fields.

"Send the Ark to another city!" the people cried. When the Ark arrived in that city, the people there got sick, also.

They sent the Ark to a third city, and the people there got sick. They demanded, "Send the Ark of God back to its own place, or we'll all die!"

At the advice of their priests, the Philistines built a new cart. They placed the Ark on it and a chest with the gold models of their plagues inside. They took two cows away from their newborn calves and penned up the calves. Then they hitched the mother cows to the cart.

"Let the cows go where they choose," the priests said, "but watch them. If they take the Ark back to its own land, we'll know that the Hebrews' God caused our troubles."

The cows had never been yoked up before, but they pulled the cart easily. They left their babies and headed straight for the land of the Hebrews. Mooing all the way, they didn't turn to the right or the left. In a field near a Hebrew city, the harvesters saw the Ark. "The Ark of God has returned!" they shouted. Then the watching Philistines knew that indeed the God of the Hebrews was a powerful God.

⊢HOW THIS ANIMAL TALE CAN HELP YOU⊣

The Hebrews trusted the Ark to save them on the battlefield—not God Himself. God looks at our hearts and knows our thoughts. If we trust in an object or in something we do, we can't expect Him to help us. Don't let anything come between you and God. Believe in Jesus as Savior and love Him with all your heart. Then He will be present to help you and bless you.

⊢HOW TO FIND GOD'S HELP⊣

Below are two special things you can do to receive God's help. To discover what they are, fill the blanks by using the code on the clock. Then read Psalm 119:16 and Psalm 5:3. This is trusting in God, not in things or our deeds.

$\overline{7}$ $\overline{2}$ $\overline{10}$ $\overline{4}$ $\overline{12}$ $\overline{9}$ $\overline{2}$ $\overline{1}$ $\overline{8}$ $\overline{1}$ $\overline{3}$ $\overline{2}$

$\overline{10}$ $\overline{5}$ $\overline{4}$ $\overline{11}$ $\overline{7}$ $\overline{10}$ $\overline{6}$ $\overline{2}$ $\overline{10}$ $\overline{7}$ $\overline{3}$ $\overline{6}$

$\overline{8}$ $\overline{5}$ $\overline{12}$ $\overline{9}$ $\overline{2}$ $\overline{4}$ $\overline{10}$ $\overline{6}$.

23
LOST DONKEYS, BLEATING SHEEP & LOWING CATTLE

"What is this bleating of sheep in my ears? What is this lowing of cattle that I hear?"

—1 Samuel 15:14

"I really love God," Jeff bragged to his friend. "I put fifty cents in the offering plate at church this morning." But Jeff didn't mention that the fifty cents was a part of a five-dollar bill he had stolen. Do you think God was pleased with Jeff's gift?

Can people cover up their bad deeds by doing some good deeds? Suppose you weigh your good and bad deeds on a scale. If the good outweighs the bad, will you be okay in God's sight? Find the answer in this animal tale.

ANIMAL FACTS
⊢Lost Donkeys, Bleating Sheep
& Lowing Cattle⊣

⊢Lost Donkeys⊣

Would a donkey owner hunt down his lost donkeys? In Old Testament times, owning a large number of donkeys was considered a sign of wealth. They did heavy farm work and were also used for riding. Some people decorated their donkeys with beads and bright ribbons. In times of peace, even kings preferred riding on the gentle donkey. If some donkeys got lost, their owners would surely hunt for them.

⊢Bleating Sheep⊣

What is a bleating sheep? To bleat is to cry, "Baa, baa." Sheep were greatly used in the Hebrews' sacrificial offerings to God. Fat tailed sheep were prized, because people used the whole fat tail as a burnt offering to God.

⊢Lowing Cattle⊣

What are lowing cattle? A lowing cow is one that is calling, "Moo." Bulls, cows, calves, and oxen were all used in sacrifices to God.

BIBLE ANIMAL TALE
⊢WHAT IS THIS BLEATING OF SHEEP AND LOWING OF CATTLE?⊣
(1 SAMUEL 9:1–27; 10:1–26; 15:1–35)

"Our donkeys are lost. Take one of the servants and go look for them," Kish said to Saul, his son. Saul and the servant walked through the hill country and beyond, but they did not find the donkeys.

Finally Saul said to his servant, "Let's go home. My father will stop thinking about the donkeys and will start worrying about us."

"Maybe the prophet in this town can tell us where the donkeys are," said the servant.

The day before, God had told the prophet, Samuel, "I will send a man to you tomorrow. Anoint him to be the king of Israel. The people are crying for Me to give them a king." When Saul arrived, Samuel knew this was the man God meant. He anointed him with oil. Later, he brought Saul before the people and told them that he was their king.

Saul was tall and good-looking. "Long live the king!" the happy people shouted. Saul ruled over Israel for 42 years.

When the Israelites were at war with the Amalekites, Samuel said to King Saul, "When God helps you to defeat the Amalekites, don't take anything for yourselves that belongs to them." Saul marched with his soldiers against the Amalekites and defeated them. But he took some of the best sheep and cows with him as he returned home.

Samuel met Saul on his way back. Saul said to Samuel, "The Lord bless you! I have done what the Lord told me to do."

"What then is this bleating of sheep in my ears?" asked Samuel. "What is this lowing of cattle I hear?"

Saul replied, "The soldiers spared some of the best of the sheep and cattle to sacrifice to God."

"Stop!" Samuel said. "Why didn't you obey God? Why did you pounce on the plunder and do evil?"

"But I did obey God," Saul said. "I brought the sheep and cattle to sacrifice to God."

"To obey is better than sacrifice," Samuel told Saul. "Now the Lord has rejected you as king." Later, King Saul was killed in a battle, and another man became the king.

⊢HOW THIS ANIMAL TALE CAN HELP YOU⊣

Giving a special gift to God won't make Him forget about the times we have disobeyed Him. Sinners can have all their sins forgiven by believing in Jesus as Savior. (See the last page of this book.) Christians who have disobeyed God must confess that sin to Him, and He will forgive them. God loves to receive gifts from those who obey Him. To obey is better then giving Him gifts.

⊢WHAT DELIGHTS THE LORD⊣

Below is a question that Samuel asked Saul. Use the words in all capital letters in the question to fill the blanks around the word "obedience" in the acrostic puzzle.

"DOES the LORD DELIGHT in BURNT OFFERINGS AND SACRIFICES as much as in OBEYING the VOICE of the Lord?"

O __ __ __ __ __ __ __ __

B __ __ __ __

__ __ E __ __ __ __

__ __ __ D

__ __ I __ __

__ E __ __ __ __ __

__ N __

__ __ C __ __ __ __ __ __ __

__ __ E __

Find the answer to this question in Samuel's last speech to Saul in the Bible story. Write it here: "_____ _____ _____ _____ _____ _____."

24
A Brave Boy Kills a Bear, a Lion & a Giant

"The Lord who delivered me from the paw of the lion and the paw of the bear will deliver me from the hand of this Philistine."
—1 Samuel 17:37

"You're a nerd! You're so not with it! You're chicken!" Those words all mean one thing—you're not behaving like the "in" crowd. You aren't "cool." Often kids may tell you some of these things if you won't join them in doing something wrong.

It takes real courage to stand up for what's right when other kids make fun of you. It's a temptation to go along with them so they will be your friends.

If you make up your mind to do right, though, you have a powerful Friend who will give you courage. He gave much courage to a sixteen-year-old boy who faced a lion, a bear, and a giant.

ANIMAL FACTS
⊢LIONS & BEARS⊣

⊢LIONS⊣

Did lions live in the land of Israel? Yes. They were the most dangerous beasts in that land.

Were lions man killers? Not usually; but if one ever ate a person, he was a threat to people from then on. One swat from a lion's paw can kill.

What do lions eat? They eat the meat of other animals. They hunt mostly at night, but hunger may cause them to hunt their prey in the daytime.

⊢BEARS⊣

Did bears live in the land of Israel? Yes. They were once abundant there.

Are bears harmful to people? They can be friendly, but they can also be extremely dangerous.

What do bears eat? They like fruits and berries, but they will also eat meat.

BIBLE ANIMAL TALE
—I'LL GIVE YOUR FLESH
TO THE BIRDS AND THE BEASTS!—
(1 SAMUEL 17:1–54)

Sixteen-year-old David took care of his father's sheep. One day a lion sneaked up, grabbed a lamb in its mouth, and ran away. David leaped into action. He chased the lion, struck it, and took the lamb out of its mouth. When the lion came after David, he seized it by its beard, struck it, and killed it.

Another time a bear took a lamb and ran away with it. David saved the lamb by doing what he had done with the lion. How could this young fellow be so brave? He trusted God to take care of him and help him do the right thing.

Not far away, the Philistines had gathered their forces to fight the Hebrews. The Philistines drew up a battle line on one hill. King Saul, with the Hebrew army, lined up on another hill. Each day Goliath, a Philistine giant, came into the valley between the hills. He was nine feet tall and wore bronze armor.

"Choose a man to come and fight me!" Goliath challenged the Hebrews. "If he kills me, we will be your servants. If I kill him, you will be our servants." Not one Hebrew soldier dared to fight Goliath.

David's father sent David with food for his brothers, who were soldiers in Saul's army. David saw the giant and heard his words. He told King Saul, "I will fight the giant."

"You're only a boy," Saul told him. You can't fight the giant."

David told him about the lion and bear he had killed. "The Lord who delivered me from the paw of the lion and the bear will deliver me from this Philistine," David said. So King Saul let him go.

David got five smooth stones from a stream and put them in his pouch. With his sling in his hand, he faced the giant. "Am I a dog, that you come at me with sticks?" roared the giant. "I'll give your flesh to the birds of the air and the beasts of the field!"

"I come against you in the name of the Lord Almighty," David said bravely. "Today I will give the carcasses of the Philistine army to the birds of the air and the beasts of the earth. The whole world will know there is a God in Israel."

David ran to meet the giant. He slung a stone, and it struck Goliath. It sank into his forehead, and he fell face down. David took Goliath's own sword and killed him. Then he cut off his head. When the Philistines saw that their hero was dead, they turned and ran away. The Hebrews chased them and won a great victory.

⊷HOW THIS ANIMAL TALE CAN HELP YOU⊷

How did David have the courage to kill the lion, the bear, and the giant? He trusted God to help him. You will probably never have to fight ferocious animals or a giant. You do have a fierce enemy, though. "Be self-controlled and alert. Your enemy the devil prowls around like a roaring lion looking for someone to devour. Resist him, standing firm in the faith" (1 Peter 5:8,9).

When other kids ask you to do something wrong, it takes real courage to say no. The devil will tempt you to give in and go along with the crowd. How can you resist him? Silently ask God to help you. Then do the right thing. David wrote some words in Psalm 56:3 and 4 that will encourage you: "When I am afraid, I will trust in you. In God, whose word I praise, in God I trust; I will not be afraid. What can mortal man do to me?"

⊢A PROMISE FROM GOD TO HELP YOU SAY NO TO EVIL⊣

Fit words from the list below to fill the blanks in a wonderful promise from God. When you remember this promise, it will help you say no to doing wrong.

righteous	dismayed	not	God
I	strengthen	with	uphold
help	am	Do	fear
hand	right	be	

"___ ___ not ___ ___ ___ ___, for ___ am ___ ___ ___ ___ you;

do ___ ___ ___ ___ ___ ___ ___ ___ ___ ___ ___ ___,

for I ___ ___ your ___ ___ ___.

I will ___ ___ ___ ___ ___ ___ ___ ___ ___ ___ you and

___ ___ ___ ___ you; I will ___ ___ ___ ___ ___ ___

you with my ___ ___ ___ ___ ___ ___ ___ ___ ___

___ ___ ___ ___ ___ ___ ___ ___ ___."

—Isaiah 41:10

25
THE LITTLE
PET LAMB

"The poor man had nothing except one little ewe lamb he had bought. He raised it, and it grew up with him and his children"
—2 Samuel 11-12

Michael felt awful. He had stolen some money and lied about it. What's going to happen to me? he wondered. Maybe God will punish me. Maybe He won't even let me go to heaven.

Michael was a Christian. What should a sinning Christian do to make things right with God and with those he or she has wronged? This devotion contains a story within a story that helped King David know what to do when he sinned. It is the story of a little pet lamb.

ANIMAL FACTS
⊢A FIELD OF MANY SHEEP &
A HOUSE WITH ONE LITTLE LAMB⊣

Did Bible shepherds love their sheep? Yes, many good shepherds did. They called each sheep by its name. They took good care of their sheep. In Psalm 23, David wrote, "The Lord is my shepherd." Then he named the good things that shepherds do for their sheep. He said God cares for us like that.

Did a shepherd and his family ever make a pet out of a lamb? They may have. In the "story within a story" in this animal tale, a family had made a pet out of their one little lamb.

BIBLE ANIMAL TALE
⊢A RICH MAN STEALS
HIS NEIGHBOR'S PET LAMB⊣
(2 SAMUEL 11–12)

After King Saul died, David became the king of Israel. He was a good man who loved the Lord with his whole heart. David helped his people win many battles with their enemies. One time, though, when his army went to war, David stayed home. In the evening, he walked around on the roof of his palace. He looked down and saw a beautiful woman.

David sent someone to find out about her. "She is Bathsheba, the wife of Uriah," the man said when he returned. Although he knew better, David sent someone to bring Bathsheba to him. She came, and David slept with her as a man sleeps with his own wife. Several weeks later Bathsheba sent word to David that she was going to have his baby.

David knew that Uriah was a soldier who was away in battle. David sent this message to Joab, the general of his army: "Put Uriah in the front line where the fighting is fiercest, and pull back from him so he will be struck down and die." Joab didn't want to do it, but he obeyed his king. Soon some enemy archers shot arrows from the wall and killed Uriah.

Bathsheba mourned for her husband. After the time of mourning was ended, David married her. But David's sins displeased God. He sent the prophet Nathan to him.

"I want to tell you a story," Nathan told David. "A rich man and a poor man lived in a certain town. The rich man had many sheep and cattle. The poor man had one little lamb. It grew up with him and his children. It shared the man's food and drank from his cup. It even slept with him. It was like a daughter to him.

"A traveler came to visit the rich man. He didn't want to take one of his own sheep to cook a meal for his guest. Instead, he took the poor man's pet lamb and prepared it for his guest."

David became very angry. "The man who did this deserves to die!" he said.

"You are the man," Nathan said. "God says, 'I gave you Saul's kingdom, and I would have given you more. Why did you do evil? Now I must discipline you.'"

"I have sinned against the Lord!" David cried.

"The Lord has taken away your sin," Nathan told him. "You will not die, but the baby born to you and Bathsheba will die." Soon after he was born, the baby died.

⊢HOW THIS ANIMAL TALE CAN HELP YOU⊣

Because David truly loved God, he confessed his sin to God. At once, God forgave Him. Still, David suffered greatly because of his sin.

This is how God deals with Christians when they sin. He wants us to be sorry for sinning and ask Him to forgive us. If we don't, He may discipline us for doing wrong to bring us back to Him. If we confess our sins to God, He will forgive us so that we can enjoy fellowship with Him again. He will never shut us out of heaven because of our sins. Isn't He a wonderful, loving Heavenly Father?

THE LITTLE PET LAMB

⊢WHAT TO DO
WHEN YOU SIN⊣

Fill the blanks below by writing the letter that comes after the one given. (Example: C follows B. A follows Z.)

A	B	C	D	E	F	G	H	I	J	K	L	M
N	O	P	Q	R	S	T	U	V	W	X	Y	Z

If you have never believed in Jesus:

1. Know that you have __ __ __ __ __ __.
    R H M M D C

2. Know that Jesus __ __ __ __ for your sin and rose again.
    C H D C

3. __ __ __ __ from your __ __ __ __ to Jesus.
    S T Q M   R H M R

4. __ __ __ __ __ __ __ in Jesus as your Savior.
    A D K H D U D

If you are a Christian who has sinned:

1. Be __ __ __ __ __ for your sins.
       R N Q Q X

2. __ __ __ __ __ __ __ your sins to God.
    B N M E D R R

3. Ask God to help you __ __ __   __ __   __ __ __
                        M N S   S N   R H M
again.

4. As much as possible, stay away from __ __ __ __ __ __,
                                        O D N O K D

__ __ __ __ __ __ or __ __ __ __ __ __ that might
 S G H M F R   O K Z B D R
cause you to be tempted to sin.

26
AWAY RAN
THE MULE

"He was left hanging in midair, while the mule he was riding kept on going."
—2 Samuel 18:9

Jessica stormed out of her house and sat in her swing under a tree. Her mind whirled with angry thoughts: *My parents are so mean! Why can't they let me do what I want to do? My friends' parents are letting them go on the trip. My parents say I can't go because there won't be any chaperones. Well, so what? We're old enough to take care of ourselves.*

Jessica knew it was no use to talk to her parents anymore about the trip. *I just won't talk to them at all,* she decided. *I won't smile either. I'll show them what I think of them!*

Let's hope that Jessica soon changed her mind and showed her parents the respect and love they deserved. In this Bible animal tale, a king's son rebelled against his father. Because of this, he lost his life one day while riding on his mule.

ANIMAL FACTS
⊢MULES⊣

What is a mule? A mule is the offspring of a male donkey and a female horse. It has good features from both animals. From the donkey, it gets its braying voice, surefootedness and endurance. From the horse, it gets its large, well-shaped body and strong muscles.

Did the Hebrew people have mules? Yes, but not until the days of King David. They were imported, and were not bred in Israel. They became very popular.

BIBLE ANIMAL TALE
⊢ABSALOM'S FATAL RIDE ON A MULE⊣
(2 SAMUEL 17:1‒29; 18:1‒33)

A handsome young prince, Absalom, raced his mule through a forest, fleeing for his life. Why was he there? This is his story:

King David loved his third son, Absalom, very much. Absalom was extremely handsome and had thick, beautiful hair that hung down over his shoulders. All the people liked him. Soon Absalom became very proud of himself, and he secretly planned a revolt against his father. *I will become the king,* he decided.

Absalom rode down the streets of the royal city in a chariot pulled by horses. Fifty men ran ahead of him. He got up early and stood near a city gate, where people passed by on their way to talk to King David about their problems. Absalom said to them, "There is no representative of the king to hear you. Tell me your problem." Then he added, "If only I were a judge in the land! Anyone who had a problem could come to me, and I would give them justice."

Soon many people followed Absalom instead of David. Absalom sent secret messages throughout the country, saying, "When you hear the sound of the trumpets, say, 'Absalom is king in Hebron!'"

Someone told David that his son had planned a revolt against him. David told his servants, "We must leave in a hurry, for

Absalom may come with a big army and attack the city. Many people could be killed." David and his group hurried to cross the Jordan River. Soon many loyal followers of David joined him, and he formed an army.

Absalom took Jerusalem, and the people appointed him to be their king. Then Absalom and his army crossed the Jordan and met his father's forces in a forest. Absalom's soldiers were no match for the king's well-trained forces. David's men defeated Absalom's army, killing 20,000 of their men.

Frightened Absalom urged his mule to a gallop as he tried to flee out of the forest. Suddenly, his long hair caught in the thick branches of a large oak tree. He hung suspended in midair as his mule kept on going.

A man saw Absalom hanging there and ran to tell Joab, who was pursuing Absalom. Joab took three javelins and plunged them into Absalom's heart. Ten of Joab's armor-bearers then surrounded Absalom and killed him.

David had begged his followers to be gentle with Absalom. He loved his son, even though Absalom had rebelled against him. When David learned of Absalom's death, he cried, "O my son Absalom! My son! My son! If only I had died instead of you!"

⊢How This Animal Tale Can Help You⊣

Absalom might have become king if only he had honored his father. He caused himself and many other people big trouble because he didn't honor him.

God promises to bless those who honor their parents. Do you remember what He said in the Ten Commandments? "Honor your father and your mother, so that you may live long in the land the Lord your God is giving you."

What does it mean to honor your father and mother? To children, it means to obey them. It also means to speak politely to them and to speak well about them behind their backs. It means to show them respect by being courteous. You may not always understand some of your parents' rules or decisions. Honor them just the same. Later in life, you will be very glad you did.

CROSSWORD PUZZLE: ABSALOM'S STORY

Solve the crossword puzzle by filling in the words that fit the definitions from the story of Absalom.

ACROSS
  1. The king's name.
  5. Where the armies fought.
  6. Absalom led a _____ against David.
  7. Absalom rode a _____.
  8. _____ pulled Absalom's chariot.
  9. Absalom rode into the city in a _____.
  11. Absalom was a very _____ man.
  12. David crossed the _____ River.

DOWN
  2. The king's son who rebelled.
  3. David's army _____ Absalom's army.
  4. 20,000 soldiers were _____.
  7. Absalom sent secret _____.
  10. Absalom hung in a tree by his _____.

27
WISE SOLOMON TELLS PROVERBS ABOUT ANIMALS

"Go to the ant, you sluggard; consider its ways and be wise!"

—Proverbs 6:6

Can we actually learn anything from an ant? Why should we consider its ways? How can such a tiny creature help us to be wise? The man who wrote this verse was Solomon, the wisest man who ever lived. If he wrote that we can get wisdom from an ant, we'd better pay attention!

Solomon wrote about animals in many of his wise sayings. Solomon must have loved animals, because he owned a lot of them. In fact, he probably had a whole zoo full. We know he had apes and baboons. He also imported ivory, which would have come from elephants.

ANIMAL FACTS
⊷APES, BABOONS & ELEPHANTS⊷

⊷APES⊷

What is an ape? The name ape can be used for four kinds of animals: the chimpanzee, the gibbon, the gorilla, and the orangutan. All of these live in Africa. They are called manlike apes. They have longer arms and shorter legs than a man. An ape has a thumb instead of a big toe on each foot. It can use its hands and feet the way we use our hands. An ape has no tail.

⊷BABOONS⊷

What is a baboon? A baboon is a kind of monkey that walks on all four legs, which are almost equal in length. It has a short tail. Baboons live in herds and eat fruits, roots, eggs, and insects.

⊷ELEPHANTS⊷

Did elephants live in the Holy Land? No. They lived in Africa and Asia. Ivory from the tusks of elephants was used in Bible days. It was so rare and expensive that it was found only in kings' palaces and rich people's homes.

BIBLE ANIMAL TALE
⊢WHAT CAN WE LEARN FROM THE ANIMALS?⊣
(1 KINGS 3:4–15; VERSES FROM PROVERBS)

King Solomon is known best for being the wisest man that ever lived. How did he become so smart? What can he teach us from the animals?

King David chose his son Solomon to be king after him. Shortly after he became king, Solomon offered a thousand burnt offerings on an altar. That night the Lord appeared to him in a dream. God told Solomon, "Ask for whatever you want me to give you." Imagine being able to ask for anything you want from God!

Solomon said, "I feel like a little child and don't know how to carry out my duties. I must rule a great number of people—too many to be counted. Give me wisdom to be their king. Help me to know right from wrong."

God was pleased with Solomon's request. "Since you didn't ask for long life and riches, I will do what you asked. I will also give you what you didn't ask for—riches and honor."

King Solomon became very wise. People came to him from everywhere to get answers to their questions. Also, Solomon was very rich. He had a beautiful palace. He owned 4,000 stalls for chariot horses and 12,000 horses. He had a fleet of trading ships at sea, along with other ships. Once every three years his ships returned, bringing him gold, silver, ivory, apes, and baboons.

God used Solomon to pass along some of his wisdom in the Bible. His sayings are in Proverbs, Ecclesiastes, Song of Solomon, and some Psalms. Here are a few of his Proverbs about animals:

Go to the ant, you sluggard; consider its ways and be wise! (Ants are busy, well-organized workers. They teach us to be industrious and prepare for later life.)

The horse is made ready for battle, but victory rests with the Lord. (We can make plans and work hard, but we won't succeed without God's help.)

Do not wear yourself out to get rich; have the wisdom to show restraint. Cast but a glance at riches, and they are gone, for they will surely sprout wings and fly off to the sky like an eagle. (Don't spend all your time just trying to get rich. God will give you riches in heaven that will last forever.)

The sluggard says, "There is a lion in the road, a fierce lion roaming the streets!" (Don't be a lazy person making crazy excuses for not working.)

Like one who seizes a dog by the ears is a passer-by who meddles in a quarrel not his own. (If you seize a dog by its ears, it may bite you. Get in the middle of other people's quarrels, and you may be hurt.)

⊢A CODED MESSAGE:
SAILING ON EAGLES' WINGS⊣

Moses led the Hebrews from Egypt to the borders of the Promised Land. Then, just before his death, he recited a song to the people about what God had done for them. He said God had carried them all the way through like an eagle carries its young eaglets while teaching them to fly. Use the code to write the words of the verse about this.

	A	**B**	**C**	**D**	**E**
1	G	N	P	R	C
2	W	I	A	H	U
3	E	O	T	L	Y
4	S	V			

"Like an __E__ __A__ __G__ __L__ __E__ that stirs its __N__ __E__ __S__ __T__ and
     A3 C2 A1 D3 A3   B1 A3 A4 C3

__H__ __O__ __V__ __E__ __R__ __S__ over its __Y__ __O__ __U__ __N__ __G__, that
D2 B3 B4 A3 D1 A4   E3 B3 E2 B1 A1

spreads its __W__ __I__ __N__ __G__ __S__ to __C__ __A__ __T__ __C__ __H__ them
          A2 B2 B1 A1 A4   E1 C2 C3 E1 D2

and __C__ __A__ __R__ __R__ __I__ __E__ __S__ them on its
     E1 C2 D1 D1 B2 A3 A4

__P__ __I__ __N__ __I__ __O__ __N__ __S__."
C1 B2 B1 B2 B3 B1 A4

(Note: Pinions are wings.)

28
FOOD
BY THE BIRDS

"The ravens brought him bread and meat in the morning and bread and meat in the evening, and he drank from the brook."
—1 Kings 1:6

Suppose a bully threatens you, saying, "O. K., you dumb little kid, you do what I say. If you don't, I'll smash you flat with one hand!" A bully is often much bigger than the one he threatens. He certainly looks like he can do what he says.

How would you respond to someone like that? Would you look at the big bully towering over you, and think, *Hey, I can stand up to this guy. It will be a cinch!* Well, maybe. But most likely you would feel like sneaking away fast.

In this animal tale, God told Elijah to stand alone before a mighty king and give him a special message. Elijah knew the wicked, idol-worshiping king would not like to hear the message. Worse than that, perhaps the king would order his men to kill Elijah for delivering it! Did Elijah obey God and bravely tell God's words to the king, or did he sneak away fast? Find the answer in the Bible story.

ANIMAL FACTS
⊢RAVENS, GOD'S DELIVERY BIRDS⊣

What kind of bird is a raven? In the Bible, the word raven is used to refer to several kinds of birds from the crow family: crows, ravens, rooks, jackdaws, magpies, and jays. A raven is the largest member of this family, with a wingspread of nearly three feet.

What did ravens deliver to Elijah? They brought food to Elijah instead of eating it themselves. This was strange, because ravens will eat almost anything — even decaying flesh. They were known for pecking out the eyes of a body, perhaps to determine whether it was dead or alive.

BIBLE ANIMAL TALE
⊢SPECIAL DELIVERY FOOD IN A FAMINE⊣
(1 KINGS 16:29–33; 17:1–16)

"Do not marry heathen people who worship false gods," God told the Israelites. "They will cause you to worship their idols." King Ahab paid no attention to God's command and married a heathen woman, Jezebel. Sure enough, Jezebel got Ahab to worship the false god Baal, who was believed to be the god of the storm. King Ahab thought Baal would control the rain.

King Ahab built a temple for Baal, and he also set up a pole to worship Asherah, who was supposed to be Baal's wife. Ahab did more evil in the eyes of the Lord than all the kings who came before him.

Suddenly one day, Elijah stood before King Ahab. God had told him to go; and brave Elijah went, even though he knew how dangerous this might be for him. "As the God of Israel lives, it will not rain for the next few years; and there won't even be any dew," Elijah told the king. "It won't rain until I say so."

Elijah was not alone when he faced the mighty king. God gave Elijah the courage to say that there would be no rain. He kept the king from hurting Elijah, too. When Elijah left King Ahab, God instructed him, "Go eastward to the Kerith Ravine and hide there. Drink water from the brook, and I have ordered the ravens to feed you there."

Elijah obeyed God and went to the Kerith Ravine. Day after day went by, and there was no rain in all of Israel. Soon people were going hungry for food. But not Elijah. Each morning and evening, he heard the flap, flap of wings and looked up to see ravens, carrying meat and bread in their mouths. They gave it to Elijah, and he had two good meals a day. He drank water from a brook (a small stream of water). Where did the ravens get the bread and meat? The Bible doesn't tell us that. Why didn't they eat the food themselves? God kept them from it.

Finally, the brook dried up because of the great drought. What did Elijah do then? The next story gives the answer.

⊢How This Animal Tale Can Help You⊣

Elijah bravely stood alone before the wicked king, who could have killed him. Really, though, he was not alone. The great God of the Universe was right there with him. He protected Elijah then and all through the rest of the famine.

Now about that big bully, suppose, as he towers over you and threatens you, your dad shows up. He stands beside you, much bigger and stronger than the bully. Would the bully frighten you then?

At times there may be people who will want you to do wrong. You may be the only one who wants to do right. It will be hard to stand up and be counted on God's side. But you will always have the advantage if you remember you're not alone. Someone bigger than you or anyone else stands beside you.

God says, "Do not fear, for I am with you; do not be dismayed, for I am your God. I will strengthen you and help you; I will uphold you with my righteous right hand" (Isaiah 41:10).

⊢GOD, OUR STRONG DEFENDER⊣

Remember how powerful and able God is and you'll be stronger in standing up for Him. The words in all capital letters below are hidden in the puzzle. Circle them in the puzzle, down, across or diagonally. Read the verses.

God is big enough to FILL HEAVEN and EARTH (Jeremiah 23:24). Everything is UNCOVERED and laid BARE before His EYES (Hebrews 4:13). He knows the NUMBER of the STARS, and calls them each by NAME (Psalm 147:4). He has the HAIRS of your HEAD all NUMBERED (Matthew 10:30). He DISCOVERS the SECRETS OF your HEART (Psalm 44:21). He knows when you SIT and RISE and each WORD of your TONGUE (Psalm137:2,4). He made all things by His POWER. NOTHING is too HARD for Him (Jeremiah 32:17). He does not CHANGE (Malachi 3:1). He is the HOLY GOD and not MAN (Hosea 11:9). His WAYS are JUST and TRUE (Revelation 15:3).

U	N	O	T	H	I	N	G	E	S
N	U	C	B	F	A	X	P	Y	E
C	M	D	H	A	I	R	S	E	C
O	B	S	G	E	R	L	D	S	R
V	E	T	M	W	Z	E	L	H	E
E	R	A	C	H	A	N	G	E	T
R	N	R	E	A	R	T	H	A	S
E	I	S	P	N	L	O	R	D	O
D	I	S	C	O	V	E	R	S	F
S	I	T	E	T	W	O	R	D	H
H	O	L	Y	R	K	E	Q	M	E
T	O	N	G	U	E	B	R	A	A
G	O	D	H	E	A	V	E	N	R
N	U	M	B	E	R	E	D	V	T
J	U	S	T	Z	W	A	Y	S	Z

29
AN OXEN DRIVER'S CALL TO BE A PROPHET

"Elisha then left his oxen and ran after Elijah. 'Let me kiss my father and mother good-by,' he said, 'and then I will come with you.'"
—1 Kings 19:20

A six-year-old girl, Ruth, met a cousin who was a missionary to China. *I think God wants me to be a missionary when I grow up,* Ruth decided.

Ruth trusted Jesus to be her Savior when she was nine years old. She kept on thinking about being a missionary. At her college, she heard a missionary to South India speak. *That is where you should be a missionary,* she felt God tell her.

She finished her training. Then she said good-by to her family and sailed on a ship to faraway India. She served God there for forty years and won many people to Jesus.

In this Bible animal tale, God called a man to serve Him who was plowing with a yoke of oxen. Did he obey God's call?

ANIMAL FACTS
⊢OXEN⊣

What are oxen like? Oxen have heavy bodies, long tails, divided hoofs, and curved, smooth horns that stick out from the side of the head. They chew the cud. Oxen are powerful work animals.

Were oxen used in Bible times? Yes, they were highly valued throughout the biblical period. They were useful for hauling, plowing, and for dragging threshing boards. They were also used for food and for sacrifices.

Bible Animal Tale
—Elisha Burns His Plow and Cooks His Oxen—
(1 Kings 19:1–21)

Twelve plowmen drove twelve yoke of oxen as they prepared a field for planting. One of the twelve plowmen, Elisha, had a big surprise coming as he drove his oxen. Here is the story:

Elijah, a great prophet of God, lived in a time when the Israelites strayed away from God. As we learned from our last story, King Ahab led them to worship the idol Baal instead of God. Elijah warned Ahab, "The Lord God of Israel says there will be neither dew nor rain in the next few years except at my word."

Sure enough, God sent a famine to Israel because of their idol worship. God sent ravens to feed Elijah, and he drank water from the brook.

When the brook dried up, God sent Elijah to a widow's house. God kept her jar of flour and jug of oil full. Elijah, the widow, and her son ate bread every day, while many others starved. God also used Elijah to do other miracles.

One day, on Mt. Carmel, Elijah challenged the prophets of Baal to set up an altar to their god. Elijah set up one to God. "You call on your god, and I will call on mine," Elijah said. "The true God will send fire to burn up the sacrifice."

The Baal prophets called on their god all day, but nothing happened. Elijah soaked his altar with water and prayed. God sent a fire that burned up Elijah's sacrifice, the wood, the stones, and the soil. "The Lord—He is God!" cried all the people. "The Lord—He is God!"

"Seize the prophets of Baal. Don't let anyone get away!" ordered Elijah. The people grabbed the prophets and killed them.

When Queen Jezebel heard what Elijah had done, she was very angry. She sent a messenger to tell Elijah, "By this time tomorrow, I will make your life like that of my prophets."

Elijah ran for his life out in the desert to Mount Horeb. Then the Lord said to him, "What are you doing here, Elijah?" He told Elijah he must return to Israel and do three jobs. One was to anoint Elisha to succeed him as God's special prophet.

Elijah found Elisha plowing with a yoke of oxen. Elijah went up to Elisha and threw his cloak around him. Elisha knew at once what that meant. It was a sign that Elijah's special power from God would rest on him. Elisha understood that God wanted him to follow Elijah and be a prophet, too.

"Let me kiss my father and mother good-by," Elisha said. He took his yoke of oxen and killed them. He burned the plowing equipment to cook the meat. Then he gave food to the people there. After that, he became a follower of Elijah.

⊢HOW THIS ANIMAL TALE CAN HELP YOU⊣

God first talked to Ruth about being a missionary when she was six years old. When she was grown, she said good-by to her family and sailed away to serve God in South India.

When God called Elisha, he didn't ask questions. At once, he burned his plow, killed his oxen, and cooked the meat. He kissed his parents and followed Elijah.

God may call you to do something special for Him when you grow up. You may first learn about His call you when you are young. Most likely, He will call you when you are older. What will your answer be? Right now, God wants you to serve Him wherever you are--at home, school, church, and play. You can serve Him by telling others about Jesus and living to please Him.

⊢GOD'S CALL
AND A MAN'S ANSWER⊣

One day God asked Isaiah two questions. To discover God's questions and Isaiah's answer, follow each line. Write down the words.

God's Questions

" _____ _____ __ ____? ___ ___ ___ __ ___ __?"

Isaiah's Answer

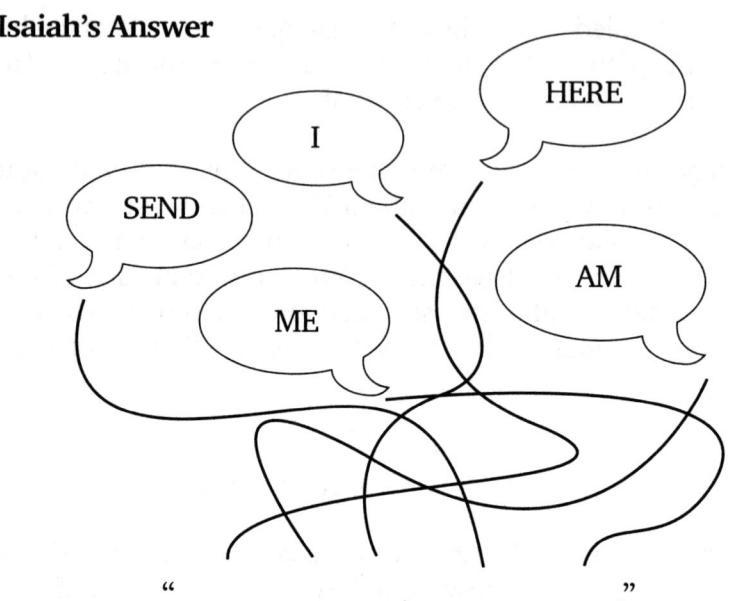

"_____ ___ ___. _____ _____."

30
HORSES OF FIRE AND A WHIRLWIND TRIP TO HEAVEN

"Suddenly a chariot of fire and horses of fire appeared."
—2 Kings 2:1-18

"Ashley, where are you? You promised to visit me every day while my foot is in this cast," complained Taylor on the phone.

"I'm sorry," said Ashley, "but the baseball tournament is going on, and I want to cheer for our team. Remember, though, I love you."

Do you think Taylor believes that Ashley really loves her? Proverbs 20:6 says, "Many a man claims to have unfailing love, but a faithful man who can find?"

In this Bible animal tale, Elisha proves his love for God and Elijah by being faithful. Then he sees a chariot of fire and horses of fire.

ANIMAL FACTS
⊢Horses of Fire⊣

What were the horses of fire? In this story, Elisha saw a chariot of fire pulled by horses of fire. All we know about them is what the Bible says. We know God sent them to travel with Elijah up to heaven. Were they flesh and blood horses? Most likely they were in spirit form—something that Elisha could see but not touch.

BIBLE ANIMAL TALE
⊢ELISHA SEES STRANGE HORSES OF FIRE⊣
(2 KINGS 2:1–18)

Elisha could scarcely believe his eyes. As he walked with Elijah, a chariot of fire and horses of fire suddenly appeared! This is how it happened:

Elijah said to Elisha one day, "Stay here; the Lord has sent me to Bethel."

"No," replied Elisha, "as surely as the Lord lives and you live, I won't leave you." So Elijah and Elisha went to Bethel, where some prophets lived.

"Do you know that the Lord is going to take your master from you today?" the prophets asked Elisha.

"Yes, I know it," Elisha said.

Elijah told Elisha, "You stay here. The Lord wants me to go to Jericho."

Elisha shook his head. "I will not leave you," he said.

Elijah told Elisha to remain at Jericho while he went to Jordan. Again, Elisha would not stay; so the two men walked on. Fifty prophets followed them and watched from a distance to see what would happen.

Elijah and Elisha came to the Jordan River. Elijah took off his cloak, rolled it up, and struck the water with it. Back rolled the waters to the right and to the left! The two men walked across on dry land.

"Elisha," said Elijah, "What I can do for you before I am taken from you?"

"Let me have a double portion of your spirit," Elisha told his master. He meant that he wanted the blessing and power of God that Elijah had.

"If you see me when I am taken away, it will be yours," Elijah said.

Suddenly a chariot of fire and horses of fire appeared. They swooped down and separated the two men, and a whirlwind took Elijah up to heaven.

"My father! My father!" Elisha cried. "The chariots and horsemen of Israel!" He stared up toward heaven. Elijah had disappeared!

Elisha tore his clothes as a sign of grief. Then he picked up Elijah's cloak and walked to the Jordan River. "Where now is the God of Elijah?" he asked. He struck the water, and it divided. Then Elisha walked across on dry land.

The prophets saw Elisha part the waters. "The spirit of Elijah is resting on Elisha," they said. They met Elisha and bowed before him. "Maybe the spirit of the Lord picked up Elijah and set him down on some mountain or valley," they said. "We have fifty able men here who could go and look for him."

"No," Elisha told them, "don't send them." They kept on insisting, until Elisha was ashamed to refuse. "All right, send the men," he said.

The fifty men searched for three days. Finally, they came to Elisha, who was in Jericho, and told him they couldn't find Elijah. "Didn't I tell you not to go?" Elisha asked.

⊢HOW THIS ANIMAL TALE CAN HELP YOU⊣

Elijah told Elisha to stay put three times. He was testing Elisha to see if he really wanted to serve God. Elisha never gave up. He went with Elijah all the way. He saw Elijah go alive to heaven, so God gave him the blessing and power of Elijah.

To be faithful isn't always easy. It means doing what we promised to do, if at all possible. If we're faithful, we'll keep on in good weather and bad, in easy times and hard times.

Our promises to God are especially important to keep. We can't make excuses to Him for not doing what we promised. He will know whether we could have kept our promises or not. In heaven, Jesus will give special rewards to those who have faithfully served Him.

⊢DID ELISHA GET HIS WISH?⊣

Elisha asked Elijah to give him a double portion of his spirit. That meant he would be able to perform miracles. Did Elisha get his wish? Solve the puzzle to find the answer. Fill each blank with the letter that comes after the one given. (For example, C=D.) Hint: The letter after Z is A.

A B C D E F G H I J K L M N O P Q R S T U V W X Y Z

As Elisha and Elijah ___ ___ ___ ___ ___ ___ along, Elisha
         V   Z   K   J   D   C

saw a ___ ___ ___ ___ ___ ___ ___ and
       B   G   Z   Q   H   N   S

___ ___ ___ ___ ___ ___ of ___ ___ ___ ___, and Elijah
 G   N   Q   R   D   R   E   H   Q   D

went up to ___ ___ ___ ___ ___ ___
            G   D   Z   U   D   M

by a ___ ___ ___ ___ ___ ___ ___ ___ ___.
      V   G   H   Q   K   V   H   M   C

Elisha took Elijah's ___ ___ ___ ___ ___ that fell from him.
                      B   K   N   Z   J

When he came to the ___ ___ ___ ___ ___,
                     Q   H   U   D   Q

he ___ ___ ___ ___ ___ ___ it with the cloak, and the
    R   S   Q   T   B   J

waters ___ ___ ___ ___ ___ ___. He walked across on
        O   Z   Q   S   D   C

___ ___ ___ land. ___ ___ ___ used Elisha to perform
 C   Q   X   F   N   C

more ___ ___ ___ ___ ___ ___ ___ ___ than Elijah did.
      L   H   Q   Z   B   K   D   R

31
MOCKERS ATTACKED
BY WILD BEARS

"Two bears came out of the woods and mauled forty-two of the youths."
—2 Kings 2:24

When a ball team won a game, their excited fans rushed out of the stadium and into the streets. They tore down signs, broke windows, battered cars, and spray painted walls.

When some college students went on their spring break in a vacation resort, they did thousands of dollars worth of damage to the motel where they stayed.

These events were reported on television news programs. We have also heard of students who vandalized school property. Many parents complain that their children talk back to them and won't obey. Why do all these things happen? One main reason is that many young people do not respect others, especially those in authority. Worse than that, they lack a respect for God and the Bible.

In this Bible animal tale, God used some bears to show what He thinks of disrespect.

ANIMAL FACTS
⊢BEARS⊣

What kind of bears lived in Israel? The Syrian brown bear lived there. There are 14 references to bears in the Bible.

Were bears dangerous? Yes, they ate honey, fruit, and livestock; so they were a threat to both crops and herds. Bears look playful and cuddly, but they can be very ferocious, even with people.

BIBLE ANIMAL TALE
⊢BEARS MAUL JEERING TEENAGERS⊣
(2 KINGS 2:23–25)

In this story, God used some ferocious bears to teach people that they should show respect for Him and His servant, Elisha. This is how it happened:

When God took Elijah up in a whirlwind, Elisha knew that his master had gone to heaven without dying. The fifty prophets who saw Elijah go up thought the whirlwind had dropped him back down on earth somewhere. They spent three days looking for him, but of course they couldn't find him.

Word must have spread quickly about the chariot of fire, the horses of fire, and the whirlwind that took Elijah up and away. Did people believe God had worked a miracle? Maybe some of them did, but others laughed at the whole idea.

After Elijah went to heaven, Elisha went back to Jericho, where he had been staying. The people there had probably heard about how Elisha had parted the waters of Jericho. So some men of the city came to him and said, "This town is a good place to live, but the water is bad. It causes our land not to produce crops. It is bad for our animals."

"Bring me a new bowl with salt in it," Elisha told the men. They brought the bowl of salt to Elisha. He went out to the spring and poured the salt in it. Then he said, "This is what the Lord says, 'I have healed this water. Never again will it cause death or cause the land not to produce crops.'" From that day on, the spring's water was wholesome and good.

Elisha left Jericho and walked toward Bethel. A wicked king had once set up two golden calves in that town for people to worship. God punished that king, but people in Bethel still kept the idols. They tried to worship the idols and the real God at the same time. The teenagers in this story most likely did that, too.

As Elisha walked along the road to Bethel, the teenagers met him. "Go on up, you baldhead! Go on up, you baldhead!" they jeered. They didn't believe that Elijah had really gone to heaven, so they made fun of Elisha by telling him to go up, too. Elisha turned and looked at the teenagers. He called on God to bring judgment on them. Two female bears came out of the woods and mauled 42 of the jeering teenagers.

God controlled those bears. He sent them to attack the teenagers. Why? Because they had not only mocked God's prophets, they had also mocked God.

God used Elisha to perform many miracles. He proved that Elisha was truly His prophet and deserved people's respect and honor.

⊢HOW THIS ANIMAL TALE CAN HELP YOU⊣

In Philippians 2:3, God says, "Do nothing out of selfish ambition or vain conceit, but in humility consider others better than yourselves." If the teenagers in this story had considered Elisha better than themselves, they would have respected him. They would not have made fun of him. Then God would not have sent bears to maul them.

If we truly respect others, we won't call them names behind their backs. We won't tease a person who is fat or has big ears. We won't talk back to parents, teachers, or others who are in charge of us. A person who respects others won't trash their property.

God deserves our respect most of all. This means we will believe the Bible and do what God tells us in it. We will never use God's name as a curse word. We will respect God's special servants, like pastors and Sunday school teachers. And we will respect God's house by taking good care of it.

WHO DESERVES OUR RESPECT

One day, when we are in heaven, we will see Jesus, the Lamb of God. Oh, how we will love Him and want to praise Him! Then every creature in heaven, on earth, under the earth, and on the sea will sing to Him. They will say,

"To him who sits on the throne and to the Lamb

___	___	___	___	___	___
10	7	1	3	8	11

___	___	___	___	___	___ |!"
2	12	6	4	9	5

—Revelation 5:13

Finish the above verse by writing the word from each box in the line with the same number.

and=1	and=2	honor=3	ever=4
ever=5	for=6	praise=7	and=8
and=9	be=10	glory=11	power=12

32
Dogs Eat Murderous Queen Jezebel

"And also concerning Jezebel the Lord says: 'Dogs will devour Jezebel by the wall of Jezreel.'"
—1 Kings 21:23

A boy steals a bar of candy at a convenience store and slips it into his pocket. Outside, he shows it to his friends. "I told you I wouldn't be caught," he brags. "Nobody saw me."

A girl cheats in a school exam by looking at another girl's paper. She gets a 95 when the teacher grades her paper. The girl thinks, *Hey, I got away with it!*

Is it true that these kids got away with doing wrong? Yes, they did for the time being. But they forgot that Someone saw them do it. God knew all about their sin. We don't always get in trouble immediately when we do wrong.

Often God waits for us to tell Him we're sorry and then make things right with others. If we don't do that, we can be sure that payday will come someday.

Wicked Queen Jezebel never repented of some terrible sins, and God let dogs destroy her body.

ANIMAL FACTS
⊢DOG⊣

Did people keep dogs as pets in Bible days? Dogs may have been the first animals to be tamed in the ancient world; but in most cases, dogs were not pets. In fact, to call a person a dog was an insult. Dogs wandered through the streets and were fierce and dangerous.

What did wild dogs eat? Wild dogs had ravenous appetites and would eat almost anything—garbage, dead animals, human flesh, and blood.

BIBLE ANIMAL TALE
⊢TRAMPLED BY HORSES & EATEN BY DOGS⊣
(1 KINGS 21:1-23; 2 KINGS 9: 30-37)

Imagine that! After horses and dogs got through with a rich powerful queen, nothing was left of her but her skull, her hands, and her feet. This is her story:

After King Solomon died, the Israelites divided into two parts, called Judah and Israel. Jeroboam became king of Israel. He set up golden calves and told his people to worship them. The kings who followed him also worshiped idols. One of them was King Ahab. Elijah lived during his reign.

One day Ahab went to a man named Naboth and said, "Your vineyard is near my palace. Let me have it for a vegetable garden. I will give you a better vineyard or pay you money."

"I can't do that," Naboth said. "I inherited my land from my ancestors. I am not supposed to get rid of it."

King Ahab went home mad. He lay on his bed and refused to eat. His wife, Queen Jezebel, said, "What's wrong? Why won't you eat?"

Ahab told his wife about Naboth and his vineyard. Jezebel said, "I'll get that vineyard for you." She wrote letters in Ahab's name to the rulers of Naboth's city. "Have a big gathering and seat Naboth in a special place," the letters said. "Have two rascals sit next to him and say that he cursed God and the king. Then tell the people they must stone Naboth to death."

The rulers did what Queen Jezebel said. They sent word to the queen, "Naboth has been stoned and is dead." Right away, Jezebel told Ahab he could have the vineyard, because Naboth was dead.

God sent Elijah to King Ahab with this message: "Where the dogs licked up Naboth's blood, dogs will lick your blood. Also, dogs will devour Jezebel by the wall of Jezreel." Later, Ahab was killed in battle. Some people washed his chariot at a pool, and dogs licked up his blood.

Jezebel kept on in her wicked ways. Her son, the new king, was wicked, too. Then God told Elisha to anoint Jehu to be king. One day Jezebel heard that Jehu was coming to see her. She painted her eyes, arranged her hair, and looked out of a window. "Have you come in peace?" she asked Jehu.

Jehu called out, "Who is on my side?" Some men looked out. "Throw Jezebel down!" Jehu said. The men threw her down, and the horses trampled her under their feet. "Bury her," Jehu ordered. The men found nothing to bury but Jezebel's skull, hands, and feet. Dogs had eaten her up, just as Elisha had said.

⊢HOW THIS ANIMAL TALE CAN HELP YOU⊣

After hearing Elijah's prophecy about her, Jezebel could have repented and been forgiven by God. But she didn't. Maybe Jezebel thought she had gotten away with her sin. After awhile, Elijah's words came to pass. The Bible says, "You may be sure that your sin will find you out." (Numbers 32:23) We can never fool God. He knows when we sin.

If you are a Christian and you sin, talk to God about it right away. Tell Him you are sorry and ask Him to help you not to do that sin again. God always forgives when you sincerely repent. If you wronged somebody when you sinned, try to make it right. If you can't undo the wrong you've done, trust God to make it right in His way and time.

⊢WAGES AND A WONDERFUL GIFT⊣

God tells us about the wages of sin in Romans 6:23. He also tells us He has a gift to give us. Many times people's wages come in an envelope. On the envelope below, the words tell what the wages of sin are. On the gift box, the words say what the gift of God is. To complete the verse, fill the blanks with the missing vowels.

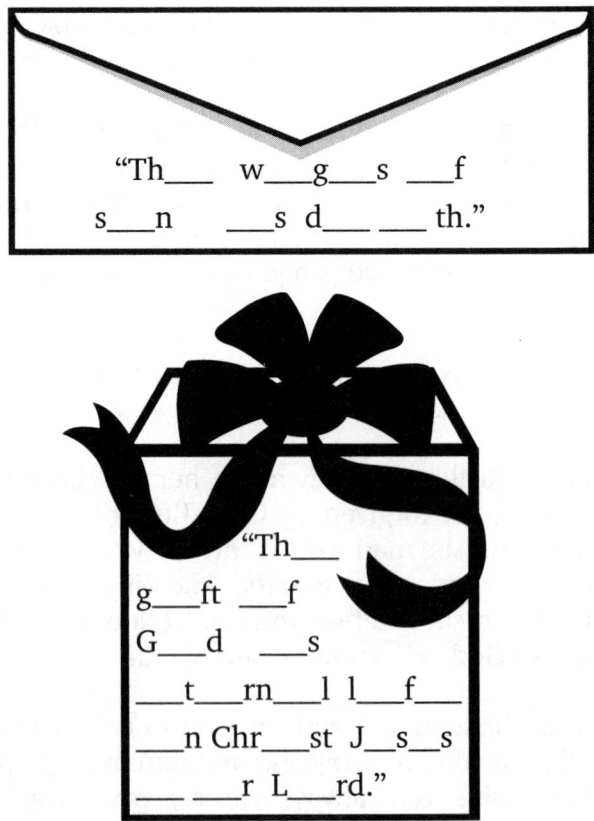

"Th___ w___g___s ___f
s___n ___s d___ ___ th."

"Th___
g___ft ___f
G___d ___s
___t___rn___l l___f___
___n Chr___st J___s___s
___ ___r L___rd."

33
A Fish Swallows
a Runaway

"The Lord prepared a great fish to swallow Jonah, and Jonah was inside the fish three days and three nights."
—Jonah 1:17

"I Did It My Way" is the title of a song that was popular a few years ago. That was at a time we call the "Me Generation." People said things like "I want to do my own thing" and "I have a right to choose what I'll do with my own body."

Is this still going on today? Yes; but it is even worse today than back then.

What's wrong with looking out for Number One (yourself)? If we selfishly go our own way, we leave out God. He has a plan for each person's life. He knows exactly the right way for us to go, and His way is the best way. Jonah found that out when his way landed him in the belly of a great fish.

ANIMAL FACTS
⊶THE GREAT FISH⊷

What kind of fish swallowed Jonah? Many people say that a whale swallowed him, but a whale is a different kind of animal from a fish. The Bible doesn't say what kind of fish it was. Maybe it was different from any other fish. God made all the fish in the first place. He could easily have made a special fish to swallow Jonah and allow him to stay alive for three days.

Have any other people been swallowed by fish? Yes, history gives examples of sailors being swallowed by large fish and other sea creatures and surviving the experience. One time a sperm whale near the Falkland Islands swallowed a sailor. He was rescued three days later and revived.

Bible Animal Tale
⊢Jonah Prays from a Fish's Belly⊣
(Jonah 1–3)

God told the prophet Jonah, "Go to the great city of Nineveh and preach against it." What? Preach to the people in that wicked city? Jonah didn't like that idea at all. Why, the people of Nineveh were becoming a threat to Jonah's people, the Hebrews. Jonah didn't want to preach to the Ninevites. He wanted God to destroy them.

God's way—going east—didn't suit Jonah. He chose to go west, the opposite way. He went from his home down to Joppa, a seacoast town. He paid the fare and got on a ship. At first, things went well. Jonah went down below deck and fell asleep.

Then the Lord sent a violent storm that threatened to tear the ship to pieces. The frightened sailors cried out to their gods for help. Still, the stormy winds blew. They threw the ship's cargo into the sea to lighten the ship.

The captain went to Jonah and awakened him. "How can you sleep?" he asked. "Get up and call on your God. Maybe He will help us." The sailors cast lots to see who had caused the storm, and the lot fell on Jonah.

Jonah told the sailors, "I am a Hebrew, and I worship the God of heaven, who made the sea and the land." He told them he was running away from his God. "Throw me into the sea, and it will become calm," Jonah said.

The sailors tried to row back to land, but they couldn't. The sea grew wilder, so they threw Jonah down into the water. At once, the sea became calm. Jonah sank down to the bottom of the sea, and the seaweed wrapped around his head.

Then a great fish that the Lord had provided opened its mouth and swallowed Jonah. He went down into the fish's stomach, where he stayed for three days. "Oh, Lord," prayed Jonah, "I'll go to Nineveh." So the Lord commanded the fish to go to land and vomit up Jonah. Out came Jonah, ready now to go where God told him to go.

Jonah went to the huge city of Nineveh. For three days, he walked across the city, preaching as he went. "Forty more days and Nineveh will be overturned," he cried. The Ninevites believed God and called for a fast.

The king of Nineveh took off his royal robes, covered himself with rough cloth, and sat down in the dust. "No man or beast must eat or drink," he declared. "Cover man and beast with rough cloth and call on God. Give up your wicked ways." God saw that the people were truly sorry, and He forgave them. Then He did not destroy the people and their animals.

⊢How This Animal Tale Can Help You⊣

"There is a way that seems right to a man, but in the end it leads to death" (Proverbs 14:12). Our journey through life is like walking down a road. Many times we come to a fork in the road when we must decide which way to go. One way may seem exciting and fun, and it beckons us to travel that way. But if we know that way won't please God, then it is the wrong way. Going in that way can lead to big trouble.

When God lets you know the way you should go, choose to go that way. You can't go right going wrong, and you can't go wrong going right. You will never be sorry for going God's way.

⊢JONAH'S DOWNWARD JOURNEY ⊣

Did you notice that Jonah's journey away from God led him downward? He only went upward after he promised God he would obey him. Unscramble the letters in each word and write them in the blanks that show Jonah's downward steps. Do the same for his upward steps. Then draw a line to connect the dots.

Jonah's Way   **God's Way**

Jonah's home _ _ _ _ (TWON) • ↓   • Up on the _ _ _ _ (DANL)

The seaport, _ _ _ _ _ (POPAJ) •

Into a _ _ _ _ (HIPS) •

Below the ship's _ _ _ _ (KCDE) •

Into the sea _ _ _ _ _ (TREAW) •

Into the belly of a _ _ _ _ (SIFH) • ↑ • _ _ _ _ _ _ _ (VENIHEN)

34
A Promise of
Two Thousand Horses

"Come now, make a bargain with my master, the king of Assyria: I will give you two thousand horses— if you can put riders on them!"
—2 Kings 18:23

After Jesus was baptized, He went to a desert. Satan came there and tempted Him three times. In the third temptation, Satan took Jesus to the peak of a high mountain. He showed him all the kingdoms of the world and their splendor.

Then Satan offered Jesus a bargain. "Bow down and worship me," Satan said, "and I will give you all this." The temptation was for Jesus to worship Satan. Then He wouldn't have to suffer and die on the cross.

Jesus told Satan, "Go away. It is written, 'Worship the Lord your God and serve Him only.'" Then Satan left him.

Satan tries to offer all kinds of bargains to us, too. He promises us good things if we'll do what he says.

Wicked King Sennacherib offered good King Hezekiah a bargain one day–two thousand horses for serving him.

ANIMAL FACTS
⊢KING SENNACHERIB'S HORSES⊣

Did King Sennacherib actually have two thousand horses? Most likely he did. He was king of Assyria, the country where Nineveh was the capital. When he became king, he beautified the city with magnificent temples and palaces. He created parks and a zoo. He even built the world's first aqueduct, a way to bring water into the city from the countryside.

Did the Ninevites under King Sennacherib's rule worship God? No. Even though the people repented of their sins in Jonah's day, they had returned to their worship of idols by Sennacherib's time.

BIBLE ANIMAL TALE
⊶GOD'S WILL OR HORSES?⊷
(2 KINGS 17-19)

King Sennacherib offered King Hezekiah a bargain: "Receive my gift of two thousand horses and surrender to me, or be destroyed by my army." What did Hezekiah do about Sennacherib's bargain? Here is the story:

Do you remember that the Israelites divided into two kingdoms after Solomon died? The kings and people of the Northern Kingdom, Israel, worshiped idols. God let the Assyrians capture them and take them away.

King Hezekiah, a king of Judah, loved the Lord and served Him faithfully. One day Sennacherib, king of Assyria, attacked all of the fortified cities in Judah and captured them. Next, he sent his officers and a large army to Jerusalem.

An officer sent this word to Hezekiah: "Come now and make a bargain with my master, the king of Assyria. I will give you two thousand horses—if you can put riders on them! Do you think you can depend on Egypt for chariots and charioteers? Do you say that you are depending on the Lord your God? The Lord told me to come and destroy your country."

When King Hezekiah heard this message, he tore his clothes and put on sackcloth. He went into the temple of the Lord. He also sent some of his men to the Prophet, Isaiah, to get his advice. Isaiah said, "The Lord says, 'Do not be afraid of what you have heard. I am going to cause Sennacherib to hear a report that will make him return to his own country. There he will be cut down with the sword.'"

Sennacherib sent a letter to Hezekiah. In it he said, "Do not let the God you depend on deceive you. Did the gods of the nations that were destroyed by my forefathers save them?"

Hezekiah took the letter into the temple and spread it out before the Lord. He prayed, "O Lord our God, deliver us from this king's hand, so that all kingdoms on earth may know that You alone, O Lord, are God." So Hezekiah made his choice. He trusted in God and did not accept Sennacherib's "bargain."

That night the angel of the Lord put to death 185,000 soldiers in the Assyrian camp. When King Sennacherib awoke, he saw only the bodies of dead men. Very frightened, he broke camp and hurried back to Nineveh. One day, as he worshiped an idol, his sons killed him with the sword.

⊢HOW THIS ANIMAL TALE CAN HELP YOU⊣

Who got the best of the bargain—Sennacherib or Hezekiah? Satan knows how to lure us to do wrong. He promises things like these if we'll follow him:

- We'll be popular, and everybody will like us.
- We'll get rich.
- We'll be happy.

Sennacherib probably never intended to give 2,000 horses to Hezekiah. He just wanted Hezekiah to surrender to him. Then he would rule over Hezekiah and his people and make them his slaves.

Satan's bargains are like that. Sure, we might gain popularity and riches by following him. We might even think we're happy for a while. But Satan's bargains always bring ruin sooner or later. Which do you choose—Satan's flimsy bargains or God's unfailing promises?

⊢GOD'S WORD
TO HEZEKIAH⊣

Hezekiah chose not to take Sennacherib's bargain, but to trust God. Below are some of God's words to Hezekiah because he made the right choice. Fill the blanks with the missing words by using the code.

	B	**A1**	**R**	**G**	**A2**	**I**	**N**
1	COME	SHOOT	RETURN	ENTER	BUILD	SAVE	SEIGE
2	ARROW	DEFEND	RAMP	CITY	SHIELD	CAME	WAY

"Therefore this is what the Lord says concerning the king of

Assyria: 'He will not _____ this _____ or _____
                          G-1   G-2   A1-1

an _____ here. He will not _____ against it with
        B-2   B1

_____ or _____ a _____ _____ against it.
   A2-2   A2-1   N-1   R-2

By the _____ he _____ he will _____; he will not
          N-2   I-2   R-1

_____ this _____. I will _____ this _____ and
   G-1   G-2   A1-2   G-2

_____ it'."
   I-1

Did God keep His promise to Hezekiah? _____

35
SAFETY IN
A LIONS' DEN

"So the king gave the order, and they brought Daniel and threw him into the lions' den."
–Daniel 6:16

Deny Christ or die! Since Jesus was on earth, thousands of people have been given that choice. Most of them have chosen to die rather than to deny their Savior.

Keep your mouth shut about Jesus. You are likely to hear these words or similar ones these days. Christian kids are being told they may not witness to others on the school grounds. This is one of Satan's tricks to keep sinners from hearing the Gospel.

What should we do? In this Bible animal tale, Daniel had to decide what to do when he had to keep quiet or be thrown in a lions' den.

ANIMAL FACTS
⊢A DEN OF LIONS⊣

Were there lions in the area where Daniel lived? Yes. Lions roamed the countryside and forests. Persian kings kept lions in captivity, which they would release for the royal sport of lion hunting.

What was a lions' den like? The den must have been in a deep cavern, with a stone placed over its mouth.

BIBLE ANIMAL TALE
⊢THE LIONS THAT COULD NOT BITE⊣
(DANIEL 6:1–28)

"Anyone who prays to any god or man during the next thirty days, except to the king, shall be thrown into the lions' den." This was the decree of King Darius.

Daniel always prayed to the true God. What would he do now? Here is his story:

Daniel was a Jewish boy who lived in Jerusalem. When he was about 16 years old, the king of Babylon besieged Jerusalem. He took the king of Judah and other captives, including Daniel, to his country.

Even though the Babylonians worshiped idols, Daniel stayed true to God. Because he was wise and trustworthy, the king gave Daniel an important job. Daniel served the Babylonian kings for a long time.

One king, Darius, appointed 120 men to run his kingdom. He chose three rulers to oversee them. Daniel, one of the three, did a good job. King Darius planned to set him over the whole kingdom. The other rulers didn't like this at all.

"We must bring charges against Daniel," they said. But they couldn't find anything wrong with him. "We'll have to charge him with something to do with his God," they decided.

They said to King Darius, "All of your rulers say you should make a decree. Let it state that no one must pray to any god or man for the next thirty days, except to you. Anybody who breaks that law shall be thrown into the lions' den. Put the decree in writing so it can't be changed, for no one can change the laws of the Medes and Persians." King Darius didn't know this was a plot against Daniel, so he signed the decree.

Daniel always prayed three times a day, kneeling before open windows. When he learned about the decree, did he hide and pray? Did he stop praying? The rulers watched Daniel's house to see what he would do. They saw Daniel kneel and pray before the open windows as always.

The triumphant rulers rushed to King Darius. "Didn't you publish a decree that for the next 30 days anyone who prays to any god or man except you must be thrown into the lions' den?" they asked.

"Yes, the decree stands," said the king.

"Daniel isn't obeying your decree," the rulers said. "He still prays three times a day." The king was upset because he liked Daniel. He tried until sundown to save Daniel from the lions' den. The rulers came back to the king, insisting, "No decree that the king signs can be changed."

The king gave the order, and some men threw Daniel into the den. King Darius called down to him, "May your God, whom you continually serve, rescue you!" A stone was placed over the mouth of the den. The king and his nobles sealed it with their signet rings. Darius went to his palace, but he did not eat or sleep.

At dawn the next morning, King Darius rushed to the lions' den. "Daniel, servant of the living God, has your God rescued you from the lions?" he called.

"O king, live forever!" answered Daniel. "My God sent his angel, and he shut the mouths of the lions. They haven't hurt me, because I did nothing wrong before my God or to you."

"Lift Daniel up," ordered the king. Daniel had no wound on him. "Throw Daniel's accusers into the lions' den," the king said next. Before they reached the floor of the den, the lions crushed all their bones. Then King Darius issued another decree, saying, "In every part of my kingdom people must reverence the God of Daniel. He is the living God, and He endures forever!"

⌐HOW THIS ANIMAL TALE CAN HELP YOU⌐

Thousands of martyrs have died rather than deny God. Others, like Daniel, stayed true to God when they faced death, and they didn't die. Either way, these courageous people have inspired others to be faithful to God. In heaven, God will give them great rewards.

Jesus said in Matthew 5:11,12: "Blessed are you when people insult you, persecute you and falsely say all kinds of evil against you because of me. Rejoice and be glad, because great is your reward in heaven, for in the same way they persecuted the prophets who were before you."

Jesus loved you and died on the cross for you. Do you love Him enough to be a witness for Him, even when it's difficult to do it?

⊢FOLLOW JESUS⊣

Below are some words Jesus said about following Him.
Beginning with the first word, write every other word in order
on the blanks. Then go back and write every word that you
skipped the first time.

Jesus said,

"_____ _____ _____ _____ _____ _____, _____

_____ _____ _____ _____ _____ _____ _____

_____ _____ _____ _____"

                                                               —Mark 8:34b

IF   HIMSELF   ANYONE   AND   WOULD   TAKE   COME
UP   AFTER   HIS   ME   CROSS   HE   AND   MUST
FOLLOW   DENY   ME

36
WILD ANIMALS ROAM IN A RUINED CITY

"Desert creatures will lie there, jackals will fill her houses; there the owls will dwell, and there the wild goats will leap about. Hyenas will howl in her strongholds, jackals in her luxurious palaces."
—Isaiah 13:21, 22

"I'm better than you." Has anyone ever said that to you? Some people don't actually say it, but they act as though they think it. Don't you just hate it when someone acts proud and stuck up? Do you know that God hates pride?

Proverbs 6: 16 says, "There are six things the Lord hates, seven that are detestable to him." Number one on the list is haughty eyes. *(Haughty means proud.)* "Pride goes before destruction, a haughty spirit before a fall" (Proverbs 16:18). God brought destruction to the proud people of Babylon. After God brought Babylon down, many strange wild creatures lived there.

ANIMAL FACTS
⊢JACKALS, OWLS, WILD GOATS, AND HYENAS⊣

⊢JACKALS⊣

What is a jackal? A jackal is a wild dog, but it looks more like a fox than a dog. It makes its den in desolate places. It has a bad smell, so people don't like having it around. It makes a long, mournful cry that is heard mostly at night. Jackals hunt in packs at night.

⊢OWLS⊣

What is an owl? An owl is a bird of prey that hunts rodents and other small animals at night. In Bible times, owls lurked in desert places and in ruined cities. An owl flies in the dark mostly by sound. If it hears a noise, it plunges toward its prey, with its claws ready to pounce on it and kill it.

⊢WILD GOATS⊣

What is a wild goat? One type of wild mountain goat is the ibex. It is gray or brown and has large horns that rise high from the forehead and curve backward.

⊢HYENAS⊣

What is a hyena? A hyena is a skulking, cowardly animal with a square snout and powerful jaws. It usually eats the flesh of dead animals that have been killed by other animals. Its eerie howl causes the Arabs to call it the "Howler."

BIBLE ANIMAL TALE
⊢DESERT CREATURES:
BABYLON'S MAIN INHABITANTS⊢
(JEREMIAH 52:1–30; ISAIAH 13:19–22)

Why did desert creatures inhabit a once great city? This is Babylon's story:

When Daniel lived in Babylon, it was probably the largest and most elaborate city in the ancient world. Nebuchadnezzar built canals, magnificent buildings, and large parks. The city covered an area of six square miles. One of the Seven Wonders of the World, the "hanging gardens," was in Babylon.

In Jerusalem, the people worshiped idols instead of God. Prophets warned them to change their ways, or God would punish them. Zedekiah became the king, and he did evil in the sight of the Lord. He and most of the people didn't quit their idol worship. They lived to please themselves.

Then one day Nebuchadnezzar and his whole army marched against Jerusalem. They set up camp outside the city and built siege works all around it. They stayed for six months, and the people inside ran out of food.

King Zedekiah and his whole army broke through the city wall one night and fled from the city. When the Babylonian army discovered this, they pursued them.

Zedekiah and his army got separated, and the Babylonians captured Zedekiah. They brought him before

Nebuchadnezzar. He killed Zedekiah's sons before his eyes. Then he put out Zedekiah's eyes and took him to Babylon.

The Babylonians took all the gold, silver, and bronze items from the Temple in Jerusalem. Then they set fire to the Temple, the royal palace, and all the houses of Jerusalem. They broke down the walls of the city and carried all the people to Babylon, except for the poorest ones. God allowed all this to happen to His people because of their sins and idol worship.

What about Babylon? The prophet Isaiah wrote that Babylon would be overthrown. This would happen because the Babylonians destroyed the Temple and captured God's people. "She will never be inhabited or lived in through all generations," Isaiah said. "Only desert creatures will lie there." This prophecy was partially fulfilled when the first Babylon fell. It will be completely fulfilled when Babylon is rebuilt and destroyed again in the future, as described in Revelation 18:1-3. Saddam Hussein began the rebuilding of Babylon, and it will be completed before the time called the Tribulation begins. (Read about this in Chapter 49).)

The first destruction did not happen when the Persians conquered Babylon. Later, the Persian Empire fell to Alexander the Great. He plundered Babylon. Eventually the proud city became a pile of rubble. At night, the jackals gave their long, mournful cries; the owls hooted; and the hyenas howled; but only a few Bedouin nomads heard them.

⊢HOW THIS ANIMAL TALE CAN HELP YOU⊣

It's easy to be upset when proud people put us down. When they act like they are better than we are, we may become angry. We may even begin to brag about ourselves. What happens next? Probably there will be a quarrel, and someone will have hurt feelings.

What should we do when proud people say hurtful things? We can remember what God said, "Pride goes before destruction, a haughty spirit before a fall." Let God take care of that proud person. For our part, we can remember this verse: "Patience is better than pride" (Ecclesiastes 7:8). We can pray for the proud person and be patient, letting God take care of the situation.

⊢Humility or Pride?⊣

Two good verses about pride and humility are 1 Peter 5: 5 and 6. Memorize them and let them remind you of what to do when a proud person upsets you. Look up the verse and fill the blanks below.

"Young men, in the same way be _____ to those

who are _____. All of you _____ yourselves with

_____ toward one another, because 'God

_____ the _____ but gives _____ to the

_____.' _____ yourselves, therefore, under

_____ mighty _____, that he may _____ you

up in due _____."

37
THE MESSIAH IN AN
ANIMALS' FEEDING TROUGH

"She wrapped him in cloths and placed him in a manger."

—Luke 2:7

Have your parents ever promised you something very special for your birthday long before the date? Did you think your birthday would never come? When your birthday came, did you get exactly what you expected to get?

When Adam and Eve sinned, God promised to send a Savior someday. All through the Old Testament, God repeated this promise. The Jews waited and waited. Some gave up hope and said the Savior wasn't coming.

Most Jews expected the Savior to come as a great king, whom they called the Messiah. They thought the Messiah would deliver them from their enemies who ruled over them. They didn't expect a baby, born in a stable and lying in an animals' feeding trough.

ANIMAL FACTS
⊢AN ANIMALS' STABLE AND FEEDING TROUGH⊣

⊢A STABLE⊣

What was a stable in Bible days? It was a place where animals were kept. A stable was often connected to the house where people lived.

Where was the stable of Jesus' birth? We don't know for sure. Perhaps it was near the inn, where there was no room for Joseph and Mary. A Bible teacher who lived not long after Jesus was on earth said the stable was in a cavern, connected to the inn.

⊢A MANGER⊣

What is a manger? A manger is a feeding trough for sheep, donkeys or cattle. In Bible days, some mangers were made of clay mixed with straw. Some were carved in the rock walls of caverns.

BIBLE ANIMAL TALE
⊢FROM A THRONE IN GLORY TO AN ANIMALS' STABLE ⊣
(MATTHEW 1:18–25; LUKE 2:1–20)

God the Son lived in heaven with God the Father and God the Holy Spirit. He had lived there forever, for God has no beginning. When God created the heavens and the earth and all things on earth, including people, He knew that people would sin. That is why He planned for a Savior to come and die for the sins of the world. God the Son would be that Savior.

One day an angel appeared to Mary, a young virgin. "Greetings, you who are highly favored!" said the angel. "The Lord is with you."

Startled, Mary wondered what the angel meant. "Don't be afraid, Mary," the angel told her. "You have found favor with God. He will give you a Son. Give Him the name, 'Jesus.' He will be called the Son of the Most High."

"How can this happen?" Mary asked. "I am a virgin."

"The Holy Spirit will come upon you, and the power of the Most High will overshadow you," Gabriel answered. "This holy Child will be the Son of God."

Joseph learned that Mary was going to have a baby. He wondered if he should still plan to marry her. Then an angel appeared to him in a dream and told him to take Mary home as his wife. The angel explained that the Holy Spirit had given

Mary her child. Joseph took Mary home as his wife, but he did not sleep with her before Jesus was born.

It was almost time for Jesus' birth. The Roman emperor issued a decree that all people in the Roman Empire must register for a census. Joseph and Mary went from Nazareth to Bethlehem to register.

They couldn't get a room in the inn. It was already crowded. So Joseph and Mary went to a stable for the night. There, Jesus was born. Mary tenderly wrapped Him in cloths and laid Him in the manger. Jesus was still God, but now He was also a human being.

The Son of God had stepped down from His glorious throne. He had left the splendor of heaven to become a man. When He opened His eyes on earth, He was in a dirty, dark stable. Now He wasn't sitting on a throne; He lay in an animal's feeding trough. He no longer heard the beautiful voices of thousands of angels. Instead, He most likely heard the baa of a sheep, the moo of a cow, and the heehaw of a donkey.

⊢How This Animal Tale Can Help You⊣

Why was Jesus willing to leave heaven and come to earth? He knew we could never save ourselves from our sins. He knew that only a perfect, sinless person could die for the sins of others. This meant He would have to die, and He willingly came to do it. Why? Because He loved us so much that He didn't want us to be punished for our sins.

Jesus knew you would be born. He knew you would sin. He died for your sins and took your punishment. He rose again from the dead, and now He wants to come into your heart (life) and wash away your sins with His blood. Have you asked

Him to do this? If not, would you like to do it? *(See the last page of this book.)*

⊢MATCH THE PROMISES TO THE EVENTS⊣

First, look up and read the New Testament references that tell about some events in Jesus' life. Draw a line from each reference to the event that it describes. Next, look up and read the Old Testament references and draw a line from each one to the event that it prophesies will occur. You will see that, many years before things took place, God said they would happen.

OLD TESTAMENT

Isaiah 7:14	Micah 5:2	Psalm 41:9	Psalm 22:16	Psalm 49:15

Jesus was born in Bethlehem	Jesus arose from the dead	Nails pierced Jesus' hands and feet	Immanuel (Jesus) was born to the Virgin Mary	Judas betrayed Jesus

John 19:37	John 13:18,26	Matthew 1:23	Matthew 2:6	Matthew 28:6,7

NEW TESTAMENT

38
THE ANGEL'S MESSAGE TO KEEPERS OF SHEEP

"And there were shepherds living out in the fields near by, keeping watch over their flocks at night."
—Luke 2: 8

"I have good news for you!" Those are great words! We like to hear good news, especially if it's something we've waited a long time to hear. Maybe your mom tells you she has bought the new furniture for your room you've been wanting. Maybe your dad tells you he has finally found time to take you to a ballgame. Or maybe the school athletic coach tells you he has a place for you on the ball team.

All those things would be great good news. Would you tell this good news to your family and friends? One night an angel brought some good news that people had waited for thousands of years to hear. The people who heard the news spread it far and wide. The angel did not bring this news to a king in his palace; he brought it to some lowly shepherds who were watching their sheep.

ANIMAL FACTS
⊢BETHLEHEM SHEPHERDS AND THEIR SHEEP⊣

Did shepherds always take care of their sheep in the fields at night? No. Most of the time, shepherds brought their sheep to a fold at night. The shepherds in this animal tale watched their sheep in fields outside of Bethlehem. Probably several shepherds put their flocks together so they could share the night watches.

Was there a reason for using the Bethlehem fields for their sheep? It's possible that the sheep were intended for sacrifices. Such flocks were often kept in the fields around Bethlehem. From there, the shepherds took their sheep to Jerusalem to the Temple area.

BIBLE ANIMAL TALE
⊸SHEEP HEAR ANGELS' VOICES⊷
(LUKE 2: 8⊸20)

On a hillside near Bethlehem one night, flocks of sheep slept peacefully. Nearby, some of their shepherds sat, perhaps around a fire, watching the sheep. Possibly, other shepherds were curled up asleep, until their watch came. We can imagine what the shepherds around the fire might have been saying:

"What a great crowd of people thronged the streets in Bethlehem today! Did you ever see anything like it?"

"No, it's the biggest crowd I ever saw. People have come from all over Palestine to register here. Why, the inn was filled completely before nightfall."

Suddenly, a blaze of light appeared in the sky. The frightened shepherds shielded their faces with their hands. The bright light must have awakened the sleeping sheep. Can't you imagine their fright and their excited bleating—"Baa, Baa?" Then the shepherds saw an angel, and they were terrified.

"Do not be afraid," the angel said. "I bring you good news of great joy! It will be for all people. This day in the town of David a Savior has been born to you. He is Christ the Lord."

The shepherds could hardly believe the good news. Had the long-expected Savior come at last? They listened carefully to the angel's next words. "This will be a sign to you: You will find the Baby wrapped in cloths and lying in a manger." Was this Baby in a lowly manger really the Savior? Why hadn't He been born in a king's palace?

Suddenly a huge host of angels appeared with the angel. They praised God and said, "Glory to God in the highest, and on earth peace to men on whom His favor rests." Then, as suddenly as they had come, the angels disappeared.

The shepherds said to each other, "Let's go to Bethlehem and see this thing that has happened, which the Lord has told us about."

When they left, they probably left a shepherd or two to watch the excited and frightened sheep. They hurried off and searched in Bethlehem for the baby. They found Him with Joseph and Mary in the stable. Just as the angel had said, He was lying in a manger.

The shepherds bowed low in worship of God's Son. Then they arose and began to tell the good news everywhere: "Good news! Good news! The Messiah is here! Angels told us about Him, and we found Him in a stable, lying in a manger." All who heard the shepherds were amazed. Were the shepherds really telling the truth? If so, it was very good news indeed!

⊷How This Animal Tale Can Help You⊷

Most likely some people believed the shepherds' good news, and some didn't. That's how it always is. When we tell others the good news about salvation, not all of them will believe it. The important thing is to spread the good news. It's up to the ones who hear it to believe.

When we spread the good news of salvation, we always have a Helper—the Holy Spirit. He speaks inside the hearts and minds of those who hear the good news. He convicts them of their sin. He urges them to believe in Jesus. He saves those who will believe. You tell the good news. The Holy Spirit will do the rest.

⊢THE MESSAGE
OF THE BELLS⊣

In the poem below, Christmas bells tell the good news of Jesus' birth. Choose words from the word list to fill the blanks and complete the poem.

DAY	LORD	CLEAR	SAY
LOVE	DEAR	ABOVE	WORD

Hear the pretty Christmas bells. They're ringing out so _____. Telling you the happy news about a Baby _____.

Ringing, ringing, soft and low. To say that God is _____; He has sent this little Child. Who came from Heaven _____.

Hear the message of the bells, "This Child is Christ the _____; trust in Him to save your soul; believe His holy _____.

When you hear the Christmas bells Then think of what they _____: "Christ, the Savior, has been born. For you this Christmas _____."

39
TWO THOUSAND DEMON-FILLED PIGS

"Jesus gave them permission, and the evil spirits came out and went into the pigs."
—Mark 5:1-20

Suppose you were very sick, and your doctor gave you some powerful medicine that made you well. Would you share the good news with your relatives and friends? If some of them had the same disease that you had, you would be sure to tell them, wouldn't you?

All persons are born with a sin sickness. No person can heal us. People who have this sin sickness can't go to heaven. Jesus came to earth to bring healing to sinners. When we believe in Him as our Savior, He heals us immediately. Isn't that important news to tell family and friends?

The most important place for us to witness is where we live—our own home and neighborhood. Jesus taught a man that lesson after He sent the man's many demons into 2,000 pigs.

ANIMAL FACTS
⊢PIGS⊣

Pigs are domestic animals. A pig's head ends in a snout, which has a broad, leathery pad that includes both the mouth and the nostrils. The snout helps the animal to dig up the roots of vegetables. A pig's eyes are small, and it can't see very well. A pig's tail is usually short and curly.

Pigs are said to be filthy and not very smart. Neither is true. Actually, pigs try to keep clean. They do wallow in mud, but that is because it helps them to keep cool. They are among the most intelligent animals.

BIBLE ANIMAL TALE
—DEMONS DRIVE PIGS INTO THE LAKE—
(MARK 5:1–20; LUKE 8:26–39)

How did demons get into a herd of pigs? Here is the story:

Jesus and His disciples crossed the lake to the region called Decapolis (Ten Cities). When they arrived, Jesus stepped out of the boat. Then a strange, wild-looking man met Him. The man was possessed by demons. For a long time he had not worn clothes or lived in a house. He lived in the tombs that were in caves on the sides of the hills.

"Come out of this man, you evil spirit," Jesus ordered the demons. He knew the awful life that the demons had caused the man to live. Many times the demons had controlled him. No one could bind him for long. People put chains on him, but he tore the chains apart and broke the irons on his feet. He cried out loudly from the tombs and the hills, and he cut himself with stones.

When the man saw Jesus, he cried out and fell on his knees in front of Him. At the top of his voice, he shouted, "What do you want with me, Jesus, Son of the Most High? Promise that you won't torture me!"

"What is your name?" Jesus asked.

"My name is Legion," he replied, "for we are many. Please don't send us out of this area," he begged again and again. The demons were talking to Jesus!

Some distance away, a large herd of pigs was feeding on a hillside. "Let us go into the pigs," begged the demons.

"All right, go into the pigs," Jesus said. The demons came out of the man and went into about 2,000 pigs. The pigs rushed pell-mell down the steep bank into the lake, where they all drowned.

The men who tended the pigs ran into the town and told what had happened. Many people hurried out to see for themselves. When they arrived, they saw the man, sitting at Jesus' feet, fully clothed and in his right mind.

The people were afraid. "Go away; leave our region," they begged Jesus.

As Jesus started to get into the boat, the man whom the demons had possessed pleaded, "Let me go with you, Jesus." "Return home and tell how much God has done for you," Jesus said. So the man returned to his town and began to tell all over the Ten Cities what Jesus had done for him. And all the people were amazed.

⌐HOW THIS ANIMAL TALE CAN HELP YOU⌐

The man who had been demon-possessed wanted to go with Jesus. He loved Jesus and wanted to be near Him. But Jesus had a job for this man to do. He told him to go back home and tell everyone what Jesus had done for him. Those people knew what that man used to be like. They listened when he witnessed to them about Jesus, because they could see how Jesus had changed him.

Have you believed in Jesus? Then Jesus has a job for you to do, also. He said, "Let your light shine before men, that they may see your good deeds and praise your Father in heaven"

(Matthew 5:16). People in your home and neighborhood are watching you. Are you telling them and showing them by your actions that Jesus has changed you?

⊢TELL THE GOOD NEWS ABOUT JESUS⊣

Follow the lines from the words on the right to the blanks where they belong. Write the missing words on the blank lines.

Before Jesus left the earth, He told

His followers to go into all the

_____ and preach

TEACHERS

the Gospel to _____.

WORLD

FRIENDS

If you are God's child, He wants

you to tell others about Jesus, too.

EVERYONE

You can't go far now, but you can

tell people around you in your

NEIGHBORS

everyday life. You can tell your

FAMILY

_____,

SCHOOLMATES

_____, _____,

_____, and your

_____.

40
The Good Shepherd & the Wolves

Do you remember the story about Little Red Riding Hood and the wolf? The wolf pretended to be Little Red Riding Hood's grandmother by dressing up in her clothes. Little Red Riding Hood thought something was wrong. She asked the wolf about his big ears and eyes, and other such things. Then she said, "Grandmother, what big teeth you have!" With which the wolf replied, "The better to eat you with, my dear!" Then he ate her up. Of course, that is only a fairy tale.

The entire Bible is true. In this Bible animal tale, Jesus warned His disciples about certain people who were like wolves that dress in sheep's clothing. He also told them about the Good Shepherd who takes care of the sheep.

ANIMAL FACTS
⊢WOLVES & SHEEP⊣

⊢WOLVES⊣

What are wolves like? A wolf is a flesh-eating mammal that belongs to the dog family. Wolves live in dens, which might be in openings between rocks, in hollow logs, or in holes dug in the ground.

Did wolves live in Palestine in Bible days? Yes. They were a menace to the sheep farmers there. In winter, wolves often gather in large packs and attack a flock of sheep. In summer, wolves hunt alone or in pairs.

⊢SHEEP⊣

Can sheep defend themselves against wolves? No. Sheep are timid and defenseless against wolves. Their protection comes from their shepherd, who guards them from sheep-eating animals and other dangers. Sometimes in Bible days a shepherd would sleep across the entrance to the sheep pen. That way, any animal that wanted to attack the sheep would have to cross over him. The shepherd would wake up, and drive the beast away.

BIBLE ANIMAL TALE
⊢WATCH OUT FOR
THE FEROCIOUS WOLVES!⊢
(MATTHEW 7:15, 16; JOHN 10:1-21)

The Bible says that God's children are like sheep. Jesus warns His sheep to watch out for ferocious wolves. Who are they? Learn about them in this story:

"Watch out for false prophets," Jesus told His followers one day. "They come to you in sheep's clothing, but inside they are like ferocious wolves. You will know these prophets by their actions. Their actions are like fruit. Do people pick grapes from thorn bushes? Do they get figs from thistles?

"Every good tree bears good fruit, but a bad tree bears bad fruit. A bad tree can't bear good fruit. If a tree doesn't bear good fruit, it is cut down and thrown into the fire. You can tell what a tree is like by its fruit. In the same way, you can tell what people are like by their actions."

At a later time, Jesus talked about sheep and wolves again. He said, " A man who does not enter a sheep pen by the gate, but climbs in by another way, is a thief and a robber. The shepherd comes in by the gate. The watchman opens the gate for him, and the sheep listen to the shepherd's voice. He calls his own sheep by name and leads them out.

"When all of his sheep are out of the sheep pen, he walks ahead. They follow him, because they know his voice. They won't follow a stranger. They will run away from him, because they don't know a stranger's voice."

Jesus' listeners looked puzzled. What was He talking about? Then Jesus explained, "I am the gate for the sheep. The sheep are people. All who came before me are thieves and robbers. I am the gate; whoever comes in through Me will be saved. Then he will come in and go out and find pasture.

"The thief comes to steal, to kill, and to destroy. I am come that people may have life and have it to the full. I am the Good Shepherd. The Good Shepherd gives His life for the sheep. The hired hand doesn't own the sheep, so if a wolf comes, he will leave the sheep and run away. Then the wolf attacks the sheep.

"I am the Good Shepherd," Jesus went on to say. "I know My sheep, and My sheep know Me. I lay down My life for the sheep."

How This Animal Tale Can Help You

Isn't it great to think about ourselves as sheep that have the Good Shepherd, Jesus, to look after us? It is comforting to know that He is always near to help us through any kind of trouble. If we will let Him, He will keep us from being led astray by wolves.

Who are the wolves? Jesus said false prophets are like wolves. They are teachers who trick people into believing something untrue. They twist Bible verses to make them say something that is false. How can we tell if a person is a false prophet? Jesus said to look at their lives and actions. If they don't bear good fruit, stay away from them. What good fruit should we look for? The teacher should:

• Believe and teach that the entire Bible is true and written by God.
• Live a life of obedience to God and the Bible.
• Teach that Jesus is the only Savior and the one way to heaven.

⊢STAY TRUE TO
GOD AND HIS WORD⊣

In the blanks below are words that a true follower of Jesus will say. To fill the blanks, print each word in the numbered blocks on the line with the same number.

10 IT	13 HOW	19 TO	2 BIBLE	16 SAVED	5 TRUE
22 I	20 LIVE	6 FOR	26 WILL	29 OBEY	7 GOD
4 ALL	21 RIGHT	1 THE	17 AND	12 ME	18 HOW
14 TO	27 TRY	9 IT	25 AND	3 IS	11 TELLS
28 TO	15 BE	30 IT	24 IT	8 WROTE	23 LOVE

1	2	3	4	5	6
7	8	9	10	11	12
13	14	15	16	17	18
19	20	21	22	23	24
25	26	27	28	29	30

Are these words true about you? Is so, sign here:

_____

_____

41
A Fish, a Snake, an Egg & a Scorpion

"Which of you fathers, if your son asks for a fish, will give him a snake instead? Or if he asks for an egg, will give him a scorpion?"
—Luke 11:11,12

All her life, Judy hated spiders and was afraid of them. When she was in college, she couldn't come home one Christmas. Her family sent her nice presents, except for one that her sister, Nicole, sent her as a joke. Nicole had found the shell of a spider that it left behind when it grew another skin. She gift-wrapped the shell, which looked very much like a spider, and sent it with the other gifts. When Judy opened that present, she screamed and ran out of the room.

When we ask our Heavenly Father for what we need, will He give us something that will harm us? Find out the answer in this story about fish, snakes, and scorpions.

ANIMAL FACTS
⊢FISH, SNAKES & SCORPIONS⊣

⊢FISH⊣

Are there fish in the waters of Palestine? Yes, there are 45 species in the inland waters and a great number in the Mediterranean Sea. The Hebrews also called whales and porpoises fish, since they lived in the sea.

Did people eat fish in Bible times? Yes, they did. God told the Hebrews to eat only the kind with fins and scales.

⊢SNAKES⊣

Were there poisonous snakes in Palestine? Yes, but most snakes were not poisonous. The Jewish people feared and hated all snakes.

⊢SCORPIONS⊣

What is a scorpion? It is a spider-like creature that looks something like a flat lobster. It crawls, but does not fly. It has eight legs, two pincers, and a long, narrow tail that has a stinger on the end. The sting hurts and is poisonous, but not usually enough to be dangerous to humans. The rare exceptions can be deadly, so be careful around all scorpions..

BIBLE ANIMAL TALE
⊢A FATHER'S GIFT——AN EGG
OR A SCORPION? ⊢
(MATTHEW 6:5–15, 7:7–12; LUKE 11:1–13)

Which would a loving father give his son—a fish or a snake, an egg or a scorpion? Find out what Jesus said about these gifts in this story:

Jesus often prayed to His Father in heaven while He was on earth. He taught His followers how to pray, too. Here are several things He said to His followers, and some more things He tells us in the Bible about prayer:

1. When you pray, don't be like the hypocrites (phony people, who brag about being good when they don't belong to God). They like to make a show of praying for everyone to see how holy they are. True Christians will remember they are talking to God, not people.

2. Don't keep on babbling like idol worshipers do, repeating the same words over and over. They think they will be heard because of their many words. Pray what you mean and mean what you pray.

3. Thank and praise God for all the wonderful things He has done for you.

4. Ask God to supply your needs and the needs of others.

5. Ask God to forgive any sins you have done. Even after we're saved, we sin and must ask God to forgive us. He won't answer

our prayers if we know we have sinned and don't ask Him to forgive us.

6. Jesus said we must keep on asking God to answer our prayers, keep on seeking to do His will, and keep on knocking on God's door until the answer comes.

7. Know that your Heavenly Father loves you and will do what is best for you. Jesus said, "Which of you fathers, if your son asks for a fish, will give him a snake instead? Or if he asks for an egg, will give him a scorpion? If you know how to give good gifts to your children, how much more will your Father in heaven give good gifts to those that ask Him!"

How This Animal Tale Can Help You

Take time to go off by yourself to talk to God each day. Praying with family or friends or in church is good, but we also need time alone with God. Then, when you pray, believe God to answer your prayers in the way He knows is best. His answer might be "yes," "no," or "wait." The important thing is not how much faith we have but to remember that God is the One in whom we trust. He can do anything He wants to do.

Answered Prayers Acrostic

The word list below gives words from this devotion about prayer. Fill the blanks around the letters of the words "Answered Prayers" to form an acrostic.

NEEDS	ANSWER	DAY	PRAY
SNAKE	MEAN	FORGIVE	THANK
PEOPLE	FISH	PRAISE	ALONE
TIME	SCORPION	GOD	

_ _ A _   P _ _ _ _ _

_ _ _ N _   _ R _ _ _

_ _ _ _ S _   A _ _ _ _

_ _ _ W _ _   _ _ Y

_ _ _ E   _ _ _ _ _ E

_ _ R _ _ _ _   _ _ _ R _ _ _ _

_ E _ _ _   _ _ S _

_ _ D

42
GOD TAKES CARE
OF THE BIRDS

"Consider the ravens: They do not sow or reap, they have no storeroom or barn; yet God feeds them."
—Luke 12:22

"Are not two sparrows sold for a penny? Yet not one of them will fall to the ground apart from the will of your Father."
—Matthew 10:29

Worry, worry! *I'm afraid I'm going to fail my math test.*

Worry, worry! *What if nobody in the new school likes me?*

Worry, worry! *How can we buy the things we need while Dad's out of work?*

Worry, worry! *I'm afraid to tell people about Jesus. Maybe they will make fun of me.*

Does this sound familiar? Worry is feeling anxious or troubled about what may happen in the future. All of us have worried at some time in our lives. Can worrying change anything? Is it possible not to worry? Jesus teaches us a lesson about worry in this devotion by using ravens and sparrows as examples.

ANIMAL FACTS
⊢RAVENS & SPARROWS⊣

⊢RAVENS⊣

What is a raven like? (For information about ravens, see Devotion #5.) In Job 38:41, God asks, "Who provides food for the raven when its young cry out to God and wander about for lack of food?" Jesus gives the answer to that question in this devotion.

⊢SPARROWS⊣

What is a sparrow like? A sparrow is a small seed-eating bird. The sparrow in Bible times was much like the American house sparrow. This kind of sparrow builds its nest in eaves, troughs, and drains of buildings and uses almost any material it can find.

Were sparrows worth very much in Bible days? No. In Jesus' time, they sold for a very low price. Two were sold for one penny. If a person bought four, a fifth sparrow was added for free.

BIBLE ANIMAL TALE
⊢A LESSON FROM RAVENS & SPARROWS⊣
(MATTHEW 10:1–42; LUKE 9:1–5; 12: 6, 22–32)

When Jesus sent His 12 disciples out to preach, He mentioned sheep, wolves, snakes, doves, ravens, and sparrows. Why did He talk about these creatures? Find out in this story:

Jesus told His 12 disciples. "I am sending you out to preach and to heal the sick. I give you the power and authority to drive out evil spirits and to heal every disease and sickness. Go only to the Jews—the lost sheep of Israel. Preach this message: 'The kingdom of heaven is near.' Heal the sick, raise the dead, cleanse the lepers, and drive out demons."

Jesus told them not to take along gold, silver, or copper or extra clothing and shoes. Instead, they were to trust God to supply their needs through people in the towns where they went.

"I am sending you out like sheep among wolves," Jesus warned them. "Be as smart as snakes and as innocent as doves. Be on your guard against men; they will hand you over to the local counsels and whip you in their synagogues. But do not be afraid of them. All men will hate you because of Me, but those who stand firm to the end will be saved."

Later, Jesus said, "Don't worry about what you will eat or what you will wear. Life is more than food, and the body is more than clothing. Think about the ravens. They don't sow seeds or reap a harvest. They don't have a storeroom or barn. Yet God feeds them. You are much more valuable than birds!

"Can you add one single hour to your life?" He asked. "Since you can't do this, why do you worry about the rest? Aren't two sparrows sold for a penny? Aren't five sparrows sold for two pennies? Yet not one of them falls to the ground apart from the will of your Father. So don't be afraid; you are worth more than many sparrows."

⊢HOW THIS ANIMAL TALE CAN HELP YOU⊣

God's children who witness for Him are like sheep among wolves. Satan hates us. He uses people who don't love God to give us trouble. We must be as smart as snakes. That means we should be on our guard and trust Jesus to protect us from harm. (It doesn't mean we should stop witnessing!)

Also, we should be as innocent as doves. If people see us do sinful things, they won't pay attention to us when we witness to them.

Should we be afraid to witness for Jesus? Should we worry about having our needs met? Not at all! We can pray to our loving Heavenly Father and trust Him to meet our needs. He takes care of the ravens and the almost-worthless sparrows. We can surely trust Him to take care of us!

⊢NAME THE 12 DISCIPLES⊣

Using the code, fill in the blanks to name Jesus' disciples. (Example: 1-6=E)

	6	7	8	9
1	E	S	W	M
2	A	R	P	J
3	B	T	H	U
4	D	I	O	L
5	N			

$\overline{\text{2-8}}$ $\overline{\text{1-6}}$ $\overline{\text{3-7}}$ $\overline{\text{1-6}}$ $\overline{\text{2-7}}$, $\overline{\text{2-6}}$ $\overline{\text{5-6}}$ $\overline{\text{4-6}}$ $\overline{\text{2-7}}$ $\overline{\text{1-6}}$ $\overline{\text{1-8}}$,

$\overline{\text{2-9}}$ $\overline{\text{2-6}}$ $\overline{\text{1-9}}$ $\overline{\text{1-6}}$ $\overline{\text{1-7}}$, $\overline{\text{2-9}}$ $\overline{\text{4-8}}$ $\overline{\text{3-8}}$ $\overline{\text{5-6}}$,

$\overline{\text{2-8}}$ $\overline{\text{3-8}}$ $\overline{\text{4-7}}$ $\overline{\text{4-9}}$ $\overline{\text{4-7}}$ $\overline{\text{2-8}}$,

$\overline{\text{3-6}}$ $\overline{\text{2-6}}$ $\overline{\text{2-7}}$ $\overline{\text{3-7}}$ $\overline{\text{3-8}}$ $\overline{\text{4-8}}$ $\overline{\text{4-9}}$ $\overline{\text{4-8}}$ $\overline{\text{1-9}}$ $\overline{\text{1-6}}$ $\overline{\text{1-8}}$,

$\overline{\text{3-7}}$ $\overline{\text{3-8}}$ $\overline{\text{4-8}}$ $\overline{\text{1-9}}$ $\overline{\text{2-6}}$ $\overline{\text{1-7}}$, $\overline{\text{1-9}}$ $\overline{\text{2-6}}$ $\overline{\text{3-7}}$ $\overline{\text{3-7}}$ $\overline{\text{3-8}}$ $\overline{\text{1-6}}$ $\overline{\text{1-8}}$,

$\overline{\text{2-9}}$ $\overline{\text{2-6}}$ $\overline{\text{1-9}}$ $\overline{\text{1-6}}$ $\overline{\text{1-7}}$, The son of Alphaeus,

$\overline{\text{3-7}}$ $\overline{\text{3-8}}$ $\overline{\text{2-6}}$ $\overline{\text{4-6}}$ $\overline{\text{4-6}}$ $\overline{\text{1-6}}$ $\overline{\text{3-9}}$ $\overline{\text{1-7}}$,

$\overline{\text{1-7}}$ $\overline{\text{4-7}}$ $\overline{\text{1-9}}$ $\overline{\text{4-8}}$ $\overline{\text{5-6}}$, $\overline{\text{2-9}}$ $\overline{\text{3-9}}$ $\overline{\text{4-6}}$ $\overline{\text{2-6}}$ $\overline{\text{1-7}}$.

43

A King Rides on a Donkey

"When they brought the colt to Jesus and threw their cloaks over it, he sat on it."

—Mark 11:7

"Praise the Lord from the earth, you great sea creatures and all ocean depths, lightning and hail, snow and clouds, stormy winds that do his bidding, you mountains and all cedars, wild animals and all cattle, small creatures and flying birds" (Psalm 148:7-10).

How do all these things praise God?

- They show His might and power in creation.
- They do what God created them to do.

Who else is to praise God? "Kings of the earth and all nations, you princes and all rulers on earth, young men and maidens, old men and children. Let them praise the name of the Lord, for his name alone is exalted (Psalm 148:11-13).

God wants children to praise Him. In this devotion, you will learn some ways you can do this. In the Bible story, people praised Jesus when He rode on a donkey's colt.

ANIMAL FACTS
⊢A DONKEY'S COLT⊣

What is a donkey's colt? It is a young donkey, the offspring of a donkey. The colt in this story was strong enough to carry a man, but no one had ridden it yet. A donkey, like a horse, has to be trained to let people ride it. Otherwise, it might buck and throw its rider. When Jesus rode on a colt, what did it do? Find out in this story.

Bible Animal Tale
⊢Jesus Rides into Jerusalem on a Donkey⊣
(Matthew 21:1‑9; Mark 11:1‑11; Luke 19:28‑40)

About 500 years before Jesus was born, God inspired a prophet to write these words: "Rejoice greatly, O Daughter of Zion! See, your king comes to you, righteous and having salvation, gentle and riding on a donkey, on a colt, the foal of a donkey" (Zechariah 9:9). Jesus did ride into Jerusalem on a colt. When the people saw Him, they remembered Zechariah's prophecy. They said, "Jesus has come to be our king! He will free us from the Romans who rule over us!"

Here is the story as the colt might have told it, if he could have talked:

Hello. I am a colt, the foal of a donkey. One day my mother and I were tied at the doorway of a house near the entrance to a village. Two strange men walked up and started to untie me. "Why are you untying that colt?" my owners asked.

"The Lord needs it. He will send it back soon," one of the men said.

"All right; take it," my owners said.

The two men took me to a man they called Jesus. They threw their cloaks over me, and Jesus climbed on my back. No one had ever ridden me before, but I knew I must be careful with this special Person. He had the kindest eyes I have ever seen. He patted me gently as I began to walk along.

Soon a large crowd of people gathered around us. They spread their cloaks on the road for me to walk on. Others cut branches from the trees and spread them on the road. People ahead and behind us shouted,

"Hosanna to the Son of David!"

"Blessed is he who comes in the name of the Lord!"

"Blessed is the coming kingdom of our father David!"

"Hosanna in the highest!"

Some men there didn't praise Jesus. They said to Jesus, "Teacher, rebuke your disciples!"

"I tell you," Jesus replied, if they keep quiet, the stones will cry out."

I held my head up proudly. I didn't know who Jesus was, but I could tell He was someone very important. I stepped carefully to be sure He was safe and comfortable. When we came into the big city, Jesus got down off my back. He gave me another pat and thanked me. Then the two men took me back to my owners. I tell you, that was the greatest day of this donkey's life.

⊢HOW THIS ANIMAL TALE CAN HELP YOU⊣

Had Jesus come to be the Jewish king and lead them to defeat the Romans? No. He had come to die for the sins of the world. He did die, but He came alive again. Now, in heaven, He loves to hear us praise Him. How can children praise Jesus? You can:

- Pray, thanking Him for His death and resurrection.
- Thank Him for being good to you every day.
- Live to please Him.
- Tell others about how good and wonderful He is.
- Sing songs that praise Jesus.

⊢WHAT JESUS SAID ABOUT CHILDREN'S PRAISE⊣

In Jesus' quotation below, some letters are circled, with numbers 1, 2, or 3 beneath them. Put the circled letters in words 1, 2, or 3 in the first set of blanks. Then unscramble the letters to spell three words in the second set of blanks. They tell what God loves to hear children do every day.

After Jesus went into the Temple area, the children still praised Him, shouting, "Hosanna to the Son of David!" The chief priests and teachers of the law got angry. "Do you hear what these children are saying?" they asked Jesus.

"Yes," replied Jesus. "Have you never read,

'F(R)O M   (T)H E   L I(P)S   (O)F   C H I(L)D R(E)N
  1   2   1   3   3   1

(A)N D   I N F A N T(S)   Y O U   (H)A V E
 1   1   2

O R(D)A I N(E)D   P(R)A(I)S E'?
    3   2   3   1   —Psalm 8:2

Scrambled letters:

___ ___ ___ ___ ___ ___   ___ ___ ___ ___ ___

What God loves to hear children do every day:

___ ___ ___ ___ ___ ___   ___ ___ ___ ___ ___ ___ ___

44
ANIMAL SELLERS, BE GONE!

"In the temple courts he found men selling cattle, sheep and doves, and others sitting at tables exchanging money."
–John 2:14

Have you ever seen children doing any of these things at church?

- Whispering during the sermon.
- Giggling during prayer time.
- Writing in the songbooks or pew Bibles.
- Shoving other children in the halls.
- Talking instead of listening to the Sunday school teacher.
- Throwing trash on the floors.

Are children worshiping God when they do things like that in church? Are they showing respect for God's house and the people who come there to worship? Find out what Jesus did when people were not showing respect for God's house by selling cattle, sheep, and doves.

ANIMAL FACTS
⊢CATTLE, SHEEP & DOVES
IN GOD'S HOUSE⊣

Why were cattle, sheep, and doves in God's house? God told people to bring these animals for their sacrifices and offerings. Some people could not bring them from home, though. They either lived too far away, or they did not own animals. It was a help to them if they could buy these things after they arrived in the city. For their sakes, sellers had come to the Temple courts with the animals they needed.

Why did Jesus drive the sellers out of the Temple courts? The sellers had become greedy. They cheated people to make more money for themselves. Also, the noise that they and their animals made disturbed the worship services. They had no concern at all for God's house.

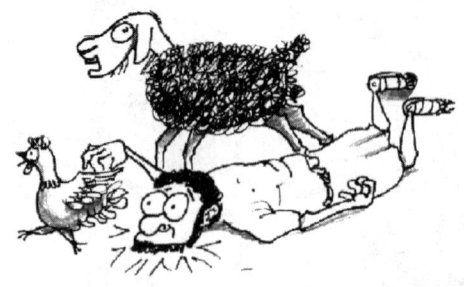

BIBLE ANIMAL TALE
⊢AWAY WITH THE SHEEP, OXEN & DOVES!⊣
(LEVITICUS 12:8; LUKE 2:21–24; JOHN 2:12–25; MATTHEW 21:12–17)

One day near the beginning of Jesus' ministry, He went up to Jerusalem for the Passover celebration. At the Temple courts, Jesus was shocked at what He saw. People were conducting business there as though it were a market place!

Sheep, cattle, and doves were everywhere. Moneychangers sat at tables, exchanging people's money for the Temple currency. What's more, the sellers and moneychangers were charging too much for their wares and for changing money.

The sheep bleated, the cows mooed, and the doves cooed. The sellers probably called out their wares, urging people to buy from them. Moneychangers sat at their tables, calling out, "Exchange your money here!" All that noise and confusion disturbed the worshippers in the Temple.

Jesus made a whip out of some small cords. He whipped the animals, driving them out of the Temple court. He scattered the coins of the moneychangers and overthrew their tables. He said to those who sold doves, "Get these out of here! How dare you turn My Father's house into a market?"

Three years later, near the end of Jesus' ministry, He rode into Jerusalem on a colt. When He arrived at the Temple, there were the animals, their sellers, and the moneychangers again! They had not learned their lesson.

Jesus drove out those who were buying and selling. He overturned the tables of the moneychangers and the benches of those selling doves. He wouldn't allow anyone to carry merchandise through the Temple courts.

"It is written," Jesus declared, "'My house will be called a house of prayer,' but you have made it a den of robbers."

⊢HOW THIS ANIMAL TALE CAN HELP YOU⊣

Jesus showed respect for the Temple, the house of God. It was where the Jewish people worshiped in His day. After Jesus went back to heaven, the Christians worshiped in a different way. They didn't sacrifice animals. That wasn't needed anymore, because Jesus had died for the sins of the world. They worshiped in people's houses or other buildings. They built church buildings and worshiped there.

The place where people meet to worship God is very special. We call it "God's house," because He is there. We can't see Him, but He is watching to see how we act. He even knows what we are thinking. Jesus was not pleased with the sellers at the Temple. Is He pleased when we don't truly worship Him when we meet for worship ? Is He happy when we disturb the service or trash the building?

⊢TRUE WORSHIP IN GOD'S HOUSE⊣

The children below are on their way to church. Each steppingstone in their path has a matching piece on the side. Write the word from the matching piece on the steppingstone. These words from John 4:24 state what the children should do when they get to God's house.

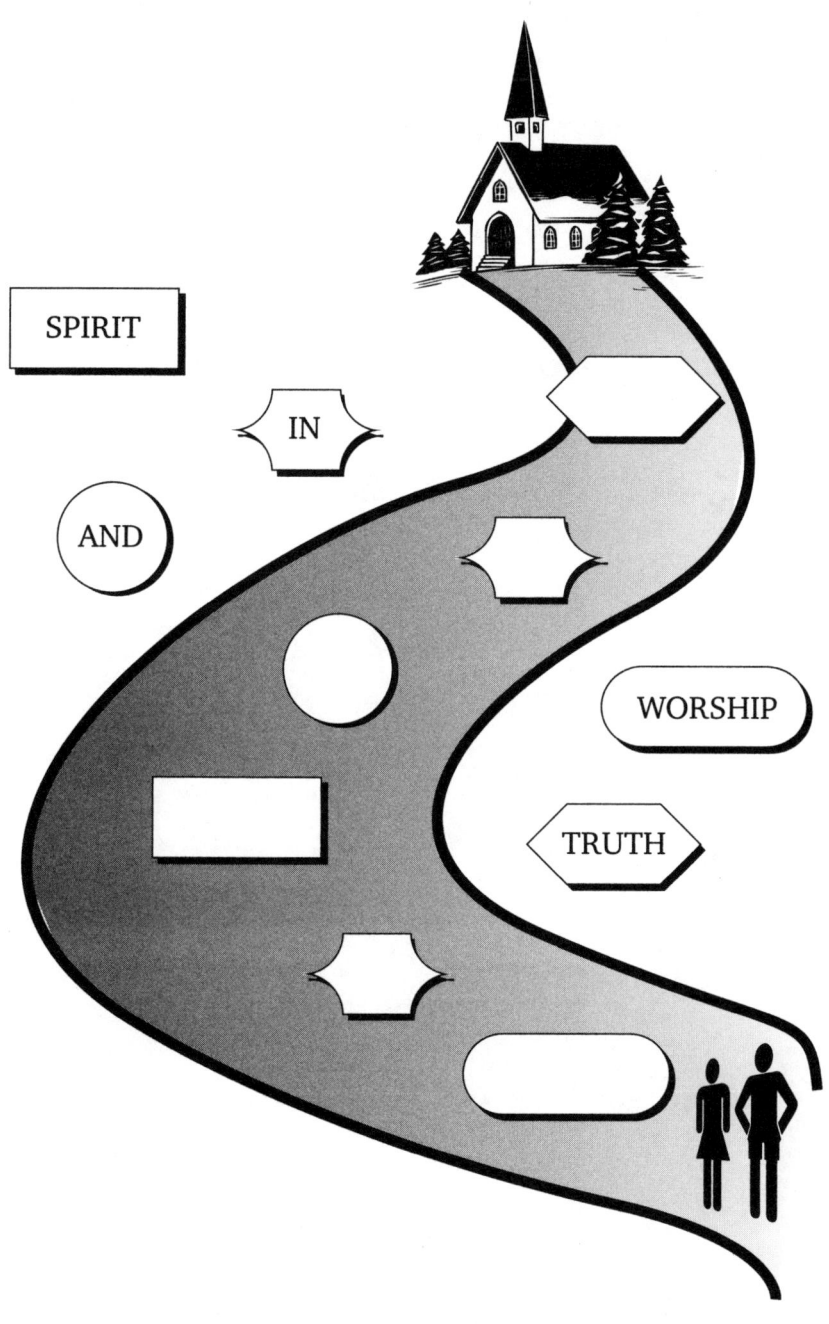

45
A Rooster's Crow
Startles a Coward

"'I tell you the truth,' Jesus answered, 'today—yes, tonight— before the rooster crows twice, you yourself will disown me three times.'"
—Mark 14:30

What time is it right now? You probably can easily answer that question by looking at a clock or watch. If you had lived when Jesus was on earth, you would not have been able to tell the time so quickly.

The first "clocks" were the marked-off shadows of trees. If the shadow was short, the watchers knew the time was near noon. If the shadow was long on either side, the day was either beginning or ending. The tree "clocks" led to the invention of the sundial. Then came water clocks and other devices. About thirteen hundred years after Jesus was here, a man invented a clock that contained many of the important parts of our modern clocks.

In Jesus' day, one way for telling time at night was to listen to a rooster crow. Including sunset and dawn, the night was divided into eight divisions. Two of them were called "cock crow" (3:00 a. m.) and "second cock crow" (4:30 a. m.).

ANIMAL FACTS
⊢ROOSTERS⊣

Are chickens mentioned in the Bible? Hens and roosters are seldom mentioned in the Bible. According to history, roosters were raised for the sport of cockfighting before hens were raised for meat and eggs.

How does a rooster crow? Roosters (also called cocks) crow and hens cackle by using an organ called a *syrinx*. It is found in the place where the windpipe splits into two bronchi (the tubes that carry air to a bird's lungs.)

BIBLE ANIMAL TALE
⊢A ROOSTER REMINDER FOR PETER⊣
(MATTHEW 26:31-35, 69-75;
MARK 14:27-72; LUKE 22:54-62)

Cock-a-doodle-doo! It was the second time Peter had heard a rooster crow that night. The sound hit Peter's ears like a ton of bricks. At once he remembered some words Jesus had said, and he felt just awful. Rushing outside, he cried and cried.

Peter's troubles had begun earlier that evening when he and other disciples were going with Jesus to the Mount of Olives. At that time, Jesus told them, "This very night you will all forsake Me."

At once, Peter boasted, "Even if all the others forsake You, I will never do it."

"I tell you the truth," Jesus answered sadly, "today—yes, tonight—before the rooster crows twice—you yourself will disown Me three times."

"No, no!" Peter insisted. "Even if I have to die with You, I will never disown You!" And all the other disciples said the same thing.

Jesus and all of His disciples, except Judas, walked into the Garden of Gethsemane. There, Jesus urged his disciples to pray, while He went by Himself to pray, also. Peter and the others fell asleep instead of praying.

When Jesus had finished praying, He said to Peter and the others, "Are you still sleeping? Look, the Son of Man is betrayed into the hands of sinners. Rise! Let us go! Here come My betrayers!"

Sure enough, Peter saw a band of men, led by Judas, coming with lanterns, torches, and weapons. They captured Jesus and made Him go away with them. Peter was surprised that Jesus just stood there and didn't try to escape. Peter knew Jesus could have destroyed them all; instead, He willingly went with the men.

Peter did not march right along beside Jesus to help Him. Scared to death, he followed at a distance. When Jesus was put on trial, Peter stayed outside in the courtyard, warming himself by a fire.

A girl, who was a servant of the high priest, walked up to Peter and looked closely at him. "You were with Jesus of Galilee," she said.

"I don't know or understand what you are talking about," declared Peter. He walked away then, out into the gateway. A girl said to the people there, "This fellow was with Jesus of Nazareth."

"No," Peter said with a curse. "I don't know the man!"

A little later, those standing around said to Peter, "You surely are one of Jesus' followers, because you talk like a Galilean."

"No, no!" said Peter, calling down curses on himself, "I don't know this man you're talking about!" And then the rooster crowed for the second time. Jesus' words tumbled through Peter's mind again and again: "Before the rooster crows twice— you yourself will disown Me three times." Why, that was exactly what he had done! He had disowned Jesus, His beloved Friend!

Did Jesus forgive Peter? We'll find the answer in a later Bible story.

How This Animal Tale Can Help You

Would you ever disown Jesus? We need to be careful not to brag about this, as Peter did. You see, we may not say right out loud that we don't know Him, but we can disown Him in other ways. One way to do this is by keeping silent. If we don't speak up for Jesus when others make fun of Him, His church, or other Christians, it's like saying we don't know and love Jesus. We can also disown Jesus by not telling others about Him when we have an opportunity to share.

We can disown Jesus by our actions, too. If we join in with those who are doing sinful things, it's saying by our actions that we don't belong to Jesus. Oh, how sad He must be when He sees His children act as though they don't love Him!

Jesus loved us enough to die for us. Let's determine to stay true to Him, no matter what happens.

Be Loyal To Jesus

Beside each action below, print an "L" if the action shows loyalty to Jesus and a "D" if it shows disloyalty.

1. Bow your head and pray silently before eating lunch at school. ____

2. Tell a lie. ____

3. Disobey your parents or talk back to them. ____

4. Go to church. _____

5. Speak up for Jesus when someone speaks against Him or Christians. _____

6. Cheat at school. _____

7. Read your Bible every day. _____

8. Be kind to someone who is mean to you. _____

9. With others, look at dirty pictures in books, television, or the Internet. _____

10. Say curse words. _____

11. Witness to others about Jesus. _____

12. Choose Christians as your best friends. _____

46
THE LAMB OF GOD DIES FOR THE SINS OF THE WORLD

"Look, the Lamb of God, who takes away the sin of the world!"

–John 1:29

Would you die in the place of your father or mother to save their lives? Do you love your brother or sister enough to die for one of them? Perhaps you do love your family that much. What about dying for someone who had done wrong to you? Very few people would be willing to do that.

"But God demonstrates his own love for us in this: While we were still sinners, Christ died for us" (Romans 5:8). All of us have done wrong to God by sinning. Still, Jesus loved us so much that He willingly died in our place when He became the Lamb of God.

ANIMAL FACTS
⊢SACRIFICIAL LAMBS & THE LAMB OF GOD⊣

Did the sacrificial lambs in the Old Testament take away the sins of those who offered them? No, they didn't. They covered over their sins, so that God did not hold their sins against them. But the blood of lambs and other animals could not wash away their sins. When God saw the animals being sacrificed, He knew that one day Someone would come to be the Lamb of God. He would take away the sins of the world.

Who became the Lamb of God? Jesus did. He was the only One who could die for the sins of others, because He never had sinned. His blood washes away the sins of those who believe in Him.

Bible Animal Tale
⊢Look, the Lamb of God!⊣
(Leviticus 5:14; John 1:29–31; Luke 22:54–62)

In Old Testament times, the Lord said to Moses, "When a person sins without intending to do it, he is to bring a ram from his flock as a guilt offering. It must be without defect and must be worth the right amount of value in silver."

A sinner went to his flock of sheep and chose a perfect lamb, one that had nothing wrong with it. He then brought it to the Tabernacle or the Temple, and the priest offered it as a sacrifice for the man's sin. The lamb died, shedding its blood, in the place of the sinner. Then God forgave the sin and did not punish the person.

Beginning with Adam and Eve, God taught people to sacrifice a lamb when they sinned. All through the Old Testament, we read about how people brought their lambs to the priests to be sacrificed. All of those thousands of lambs were little pictures of the Savior who would come and take away sins. People longed for Him to come—the One they called their Messiah.

John the Baptist brought God's message to the people that their Messiah would soon arrive. Then one day he saw Jesus, and he said, "Look, the Lamb of God who takes away the sin of the world!" John knew that Jesus was the One whom all those sacrificed lambs pictured. He had come at last!

Three years later, Jesus knew it was the time for Him to die as the Lamb of God. He headed for Jerusalem, where He knew

He would be captured. The rulers of the Jews had been looking for a way to capture Jesus away from the crowd.

Judas, one of Jesus' own disciples, came to them and said, "Pay me money, and I will take you to Him." One night, Judas took the rulers and others to the Garden of Gethsemane, where they captured Jesus.

Jesus' enemies put Him on trial before three different judges. The soldiers mocked Him, beat Him, slapped His face, spit on Him, and pressed a crown of thorns on His head. Jesus did not say a word. Nobody could find any fault in Him, yet they took Him out to be crucified.

The Roman soldiers led Jesus out to a place where they crucified criminals. They nailed His hands and His feet to a cross and left Him hanging there. It was a very painful and shameful death. Even the sun hid its face, and darkness came over the city. At the end of six long hours, Jesus gave up His life with a loud cry, "It is finished!" He gave His spirit into the hands of the Father, and He died.

But there is good news! Jesus did not stay dead. He rose again on the third day. Now we can ask Him to forgive our sins and save us. He will come into our heart and wash all our sins away with His blood. Isn't that great, good news?

⊢How This Animal Tale Can Help You⊣

This tale about lambs and the Lamb of God is the most important one of all. Before God created people, He knew we would all sin. He wanted us to live in heaven with Him, but He could not allow sin in heaven. Sin must be punished and taken away. So God made a plan. The sinless Son of God would take the punishment for the whole world of sinners. He would shed His blood on the cruel cross and die in our place. Those who would believe in Him as Savior and Lord would have their sins forgiven.

The lambs offered by sinners in the Old Testament were pictures of what Jesus would do. They shed their blood in the place of the sinners. Jesus, the Lamb of God, died for you. Have you believed in Him as your Savior? *(See the last page of this book.)*

⊢A SPECIAL NAME FOR JESUS⊢

Write the letters on the lines to find a special name for Jesus.

In PEAT but not in APE   ____

In SHOW, but not in SOW   ____

In CLEAN, but not in CLAN   ____

In PLOP, but not in POP   ____

In STEAM, but not in STEM   ____

In BOMB, but not in BOB   ____

In BREAK, but not in RAKE   ____

In SOAPS, but not in PASS   ____

In FIRM, but not in RIM   ____

In GATE, but not in TEA   ____

In TOES, but not in SET   ____

In DOWN, but not in NOW   ____

47
CATCHING FISH & FEEDING SHEEP

"Simon Peter climbed aboard and dragged the net ashore. It was full of large fish, 153, but even with so many the net was not torn."
–John 21:11

What do you plan to be when you grow up? Most likely you don't know that yet. You have plenty of time to decide before you grow up. Did you know that God has a plan for what He wants you to do? Some Christians say, "It's my life, and I should be allowed to do what I choose."

God says to Christians, "You are not your own; you were bought at a price. Therefore honor God with your body" (1 Corinthians 6:19-20). Who bought you? Jesus did. What price did He pay for you? He bought you with His blood that He shed on the cross for you.

The best thing you can do with your life is to serve God. Peter found this out when he learned that feeding God's sheep was better than catching fish in the Sea of Galilee.

ANIMAL FACTS
⊢SEA OF GALILEE FISH & FOOD FOR GOD'S SHEEP ⊢

⊢SEA OF GALILEE FISH⊢

What is the Sea of Galilee? It is a large inland lake whose waters are sweet and sparkling. It abounds with fish. Many men made their living by catching the fish there.

⊢FOOD FOR GOD'S SHEEP⊢

What do God's sheep eat? Jesus is the Good Shepherd. His sheep are people who have believed in Him as Savior. They need to be taught God's Word, the Bible. Sinners are like lost sheep. They need to hear the Gospel.

BIBLE ANIMAL TALE:
―FISHERMAN PETER, FEED GOD'S SHEEP―
(JOHN 21:1–19)

After Jesus arose from the dead, He appeared to His followers several times. In this story, seven of Jesus' disciples saw Him at the Sea of Galilee.

"I'm going fishing," Peter said to six other disciples.

"We'll go with you," said his friends. They went to the Sea of Galilee and got into Peter's boat. They fished all through the night but caught nothing.

About dawn, Jesus stood on the shore. The disciples saw Him, but they couldn't tell who He was in the morning mist. Jesus called, "Friends, have you caught any fish?"

"No," they answered.

"Throw your net on the right side of the boat," Jesus told them. "You will find some there." When they cast out the net, there were so many fish they couldn't haul it in.

Then John said to Peter, "It is the Lord!" Peter threw his outer garment around him, jumped into the water, and swam to shore. The others followed him in the boat, towing the net full of fish. When they landed, they saw a fire of burning coals with fish and bread cooking on it.

Jesus said to them, "Bring some of the fish you caught." Peter climbed back into the boat and dragged the net to shore. It was full of large fish—153 of them—but the net was not torn. Jesus said, "Come and have breakfast." He took the bread and gave it to them, along with the fish.

When they finished eating, Jesus said to Peter, "Do you truly love me more than these others?"

"Yes, Lord," Peter answered, "You know that I love You."

"Feed my lambs," Jesus said. Then again He asked, "Peter, do you love Me?"

Peter said, "Yes, Lord, You know that I love You."

"Take care of My sheep," Jesus said.

Jesus said to him the third time, "Peter, do you love Me?"

Peter was hurt when Jesus asked three times if he loved Him. "Lord, you know all things," Peter replied. "You know that I love You."

"Feed My sheep," Jesus said. "I tell you, when you were young, you dressed yourself. You went where you wanted to go. But when you are old, you will stretch out your hands, and someone else will dress you and take you where you don't want to go." Jesus was talking about the way Peter would die. From this conversation, we know that Jesus had forgiven Peter for disowning Him.

After Jesus went back to heaven, Peter fished for men. He preached a great sermon to a large crowd of people. Three thousand of them were saved and baptized. He preached the Gospel in many places. He wrote two books of the Bible. Finally he was taken to Rome, where he was crucified, stretching out his arms, as Jesus had said. Did Peter prove his love for Jesus? Yes, he surely did!

⊢HOW THIS ANIMAL TALE CAN HELP YOU⊣

Peter had more important business to do than fishing. Jesus made that clear. He was to preach the Gospel and win people to Jesus. He was to teach God's Word to those who got saved. And that's what Peter did from then on.

If you are saved, God has a job for you to do, also. Right now, you can tell others about Him. He wants you to serve Him right where you are—at home, at school, at church, and in your neighborhood. God also has a plan for your life when you get older. It may be to serve Him fulltime as a Christian worker at home or overseas. It may be to serve Him in any way you can as you pursue a career.

The important thing is to pray and ask God to show you what He wants you to do. He may not let you know what it is until you are grown. But when He does, will you say, "Here am I, Lord"?

⊢A PROMISE TO JESUS⊣

Do you love Jesus? Would you like to make a promise to Him that you will do what He wants you to do? Cross out all the X's and Z's in the puzzle. Write the remaining letters in the blanks.

```
Z I X X L O Z Z V X Z E X Z X Y O X X U X Z X X
X I Z X Z G X X I X Z X V X E X X M Z Y X X L Z
I X X F Z Z Z E X T X Z X O Y X X O Z Z U X Z I X
Z W I X L Z L Z X Z B Z Z X X E Z X W X X H Z A X
Z Z T X X Z X Y X X O Z U X X W X X Z A X N X X
Z Z T X M X Z E Z Z Z T X O X X Z B X X Z E X X
```

Dear Jesus,

— — — — — — — — —.

— — — — — — — — — — — —

— — — — —. — — — — — — — —

— — — — — — — — — — —

— — — — — —.

Your Friend, _____

48
PETER'S STRANGE VISION OF ANIMALS

"He saw heaven opened and something like a large sheet being let down to earth by its four corners. It contained all kinds of four-footed animals, as well as reptiles of the earth and birds of the air."
—Acts 10:11,12

Andrea, Janice, and Tyler walked down the street. Soon they saw a small, unpainted house with broken steps. Three little dirty, ragged children played in the yard. "Let's invite those children to church," said Andrea.

"No, we'd better not," said Tyler. "They're poor and dirty. They wouldn't fit in with the other kids at our church."

As the children kept walking, they saw some children coming toward them. "How about asking those kids to come to church?" asked Andrea.

"I don't think we should," said Janice. "They're not the same color we are."

Finally, the three children passed a beautiful big house. "The girl in that house is in my class at school," said Andrea. "She's rich. Shall we ask her to church?"

"No; she's stuck up," said Tyler. "She thinks she's better than other kids."

"She's kind of like you two, then, isn't she?" asked Andrea.

In this story, Peter learned a lesson about how to treat other people when he saw a sheet full of unclean animals.

ANIMAL FACTS
⊢CLEAN & UNCLEAN ANIMALS ⊣

What are clean and unclean animals? God gave rules to the Israelites about the kind of animals they were to eat and sacrifice. These He called clean. He told His people not to eat or sacrifice any of the rest of the animals. He called them unclean. They were tabooed.

BIBLE ANIMAL TALE
⊢A SHEET FULL OF TABOOED ANIMALS, REPTILES & BIRDS⊣
(ACTS 10:1⊢48)

Cornelius, a Roman officer, loved God; but he didn't know about believing in Jesus for salvation. Cornelius and his family prayed to God and gave generously to people in need. One day Cornelius had a vision of an angel. "Cornelius!" the angel said to him.

"What is it, Lord?" asked Cornelius.

"God sees your prayers and your gifts to the poor," answered the angel. "Send men to Joppa to bring back a man named Simon Peter." When the angel left, Cornelius sent three men to Joppa.

While they were on their way, Peter went up on the rooftop to pray. It was about noon, and Peter was hungry. In a trance, he saw a sheet being let down to earth by its four corners. It contained all kinds of four-footed animals, reptiles, and birds. Then a voice said, "Get up, Peter. Kill and eat."

Peter saw the unclean animals. "Surely not, Lord!" said Peter. "I have never eaten anything unclean."

"Do not call anything impure that God has made clean," said the voice. This happened three times. Then the sheet was drawn back to heaven. Peter wondered what his vision meant. About that time, the men sent by Cornelius arrived. Then the

Holy Spirit said to Peter, "Three men are looking for you. Go downstairs. I have sent these men, so don't hesitate to go with them."

Peter went down and asked the men, "Why are you here?"

The men told Peter about Cornelius and the angel. "The angel told him to send for you," the men said. Then Peter invited the men to stay overnight. The next day he and some other believers went to see Cornelius. A large crowd of people had gathered there.

Peter said to the crowd, "It is against our law for a Jew to visit with Gentiles," he said. "But God has shown me I should not call any man unclean, so I came without objecting. Why have you sent for me?"

Cornelius told Peter about the angel and what he said. "We are all here in the presence of God to hear everything the Lord tells you to say," Cornelius said.

Peter said, "Now I realize that God doesn't have favorites. He accepts all men of every nation who fear Him and do what is right." Peter told them about Jesus, God's Son, who died on the cross for the sins of all people. "Jesus came alive again," Peter declared. "Everyone who believes in Him receives forgiveness of sins."

Cornelius and the others did believe in Jesus. Then the Holy Spirit came on all of them. Peter ordered that those Gentiles should be baptized in the name of Jesus Christ.

⊢How This Animal Tale
Can Help You⊣

God chose Abraham to be the beginning father of the Jews, God's special people. They were the ones to whom God gave His rules and laws. He taught them to sacrifice animals to have their sins forgiven. He used them to write the Old Testament. God promised that a Savior would come from the Jews. All other people were called Gentiles. The Jews would not associate with them.

Before Jesus went back to heaven, He told His followers, "Go into all the world and preach the good news to all creation." They didn't understand that this meant the Gentiles as well as the Jews until Peter saw the sheet full of unclean animals.

God loves all people, and Jesus died for all people. Then should we choose to tell only certain people about Jesus? Should we invite only those just like us to come to church?

⊢Preach the Good News
to All Creation ⊣

Who is included in all creation? Some suggested answers are given in the word list. In the acrostic below, fit the words in all capital letters into the blanks around the word creation.

FRIENDS   NEIGHBORS   FAMILY
SCHOOLMATES   ENEMIES   STRANGERS
all RACES   all the WORLD

___ ___ C ___ ___
___ ___ R ___ ___
___ ___ ___ E ___ ___ ___
___ A ___ ___ ___ ___
___ T ___ ___ ___ ___ ___ ___ ___
___ ___ I ___ ___ ___ ___ ___ ___
___ ___ ___ ___ O ___ ___ ___ ___ ___ ___
___ N ___ ___ ___ ___ ___

49
JESUS AND THE ARMIES OF HEAVEN RIDE ON WHITE HORSES

"I saw heaven standing open and there before me was a white horse, whose rider is called Faithful and True."
—Revelation 19:11

A band marches down the street, playing your school song. Majorettes follow the band, stepping proudly in unison to the rhythm. Several floats roll by, draped in your school colors. Last of all your home team marches along. The people lining the streets cheer loudly. Your home team has won a big game, and this is their victory parade.

Someday Jesus and His armies will ride white horses in the biggest victory parade of all.

ANIMAL FACTS
⊢WHITE HORSES &
THE ARMIES OF HEAVEN⊣

⊢WHITE HORSES⊣

Why are white horses special? In the Bible, a white horse usually was a symbol of victory. Some kings in Bible times rode a white horse in a victory parade after winning a battle. The white horses in this story may be real horses, but they may just be symbols of victory.

⊢ARMIES OF HEAVEN⊣

Who will be in the armies of heaven? These armies are made up of believers who have already gone to heaven. They will return to earth with Jesus.

BIBLE ANIMAL TALE
JESUS, HIS ARMIES & WHITE HORSES
IN A VICTORY PARADE
(1 THESSALONIANS 4:13–17;
REVELATION 19:1–21)

A person is made up of a body, a soul, and a spirit. When believers die, God takes their souls and spirits to heaven. Their bodies are laid in the grave. They won't be there forever, though. A great day is coming! Jesus will come from heaven to the air above us. Believers will hear a loud shout, the voice of the archangel, and the trumpet call of God.

Jesus will bring with Him the souls and spirits of believers who have died. He will raise their bodies and make them new. He will reunite each body with its soul and spirit. Then God will change the bodies of living believers and make them new. Together, we'll go up to heaven with Jesus.

While we enjoy heaven for seven years, there will be terrible troubles on earth. This is called the Tribulation. What will happen at the end of the seven years? God gave John a vision of all of this, and he wrote it in the Book of Revelation. Here is how he described it:

"I saw a great crowd of people in heaven who shouted, 'Hallelujah! Salvation and glory and power belong to our God.'

"A voice came from the throne, saying: 'Praise our God, all you servants, you who fear Him, both small and great!'

"A great multitude cried out with a roar. It sounded like the boom of pounding waves and the roar of loud thunder. They shouted: 'Hallelujah! Our Lord God Almighty reigns! Let us rejoice and be glad and give Him glory!'

"Then I saw heaven opened, and a white horse appeared. His rider was called Faithful and True. His eyes blazed like a flame of fire. I saw many kingly crowns on His head. His robe had been dipped in blood. His name was called The Word of God. A sharp sword came from His mouth. On His robe and thigh these words were written: KING OF KINGS AND LORD OF LORDS.

"The rider on the white horse led the armies of heaven, who were dressed in dazzling, clean linen. They rode on white horses and followed the rider on the white horse to earth.

"On earth, the kings of the earth and their armies gathered together, led by a wicked man called the beast. They came to make war against the rider on the white horse and His army. But I saw the beast and his partner, the false prophet, captured and thrown alive into the fiery lake of burning sulfur. All their armies were killed by the sword from the mouth of the rider on the white horse. Then the birds of prey ate them up."

HOW THIS ANIMAL TALE CAN HELP YOU

When will Jesus come to take believers to heaven? We don't know. This event, which is called the Rapture, is God's secret. He tells us, "So you also must be ready, because the Son of Man will come at an hour when you do not expect him" (Matthew 24:44).

How can you be ready for Jesus to come in the air? To be sure you're ready for the Rapture, you need to be saved now. Jesus will come in a flash, in the twinkling of an eye. There will be no time to get saved then.

Would you like to have help in how to believe in Jesus and receive Him into your heart? *(See the last page of this book.)*

⊶THE VICTORY PARADE WORD SEARCH ⊶

The word list below contains words from the Bible story. Find and circle them in the puzzle. You can go down, across, and diagonally.

BODY	SHOUT	ENJOY	HE
GOD	REVELATION	SOUL	SPIRIT
GLORY	LIVING	NEW	SMALL
HALLELUJAH	POWER	GRAVE	JESUS
WE	BELIEVERS	WHITE	HEAVEN
HORSE	CROWNS	AIR	BLOOD
ARCHANGEL	KING	LAID	SWORD
ATE	TROUBLES	EARTH	FIERY
BIRDS			

A	I	R	W	H	O	R	S	E	H
A	R	C	H	A	N	G	E	L	E
N	E	R	I	L	S	R	W	I	A
E	V	O	T	L	M	A	E	V	V
W	E	W	E	E	A	V	S	I	E
E	L	N	X	L	L	E	H	N	N
A	A	S	O	U	L	X	O	G	B
K	T	R	X	J	E	S	U	S	E
P	I	E	T	A	E	W	T	P	L
G	O	N	B	H	N	O	H	I	I
L	N	W	G	L	J	R	E	R	E
O	A	X	E	B	O	D	Y	I	V
R	F	I	E	R	Y	O	X	T	E
Y	G	O	D	B	I	R	D	S	R
T	R	O	U	B	L	E	S	X	S

50
A Time of Peace for People & Animals

"The wolf will live with the lamb, the leopard will lie down with the goat, the calf and the lion and the yearling together; and a little child shall lead them."
—Isaiah 11:6

Which kind of dog would you like for a pet—an obedient and loving one or a disobedient one that growls and bites you? Would you like to live in a forest where wild, ferocious animals roam freely? Would you like to live near the animals if they were all as tame as kittens?

Someday all animals will live peacefully and harmlessly with people and other animals. Thirteen animals are named in this last Bible animal tale. Here are facts about the animals that haven't been named in this book yet...

ANIMAL FACTS
⊢Leopard, Yearling, Cobra, Viper⊣

⊢Leopard⊣

What is a leopard like? A leopard is a member of the cat family. It is more savage and fierce than a lion. It is highly intelligent and treacherous. It can climb a tree as easily as a cat. Leopards don't usually attack human beings. Several verses in the Bible mention leopards.

⊢Yearling⊣

What is a yearling? A yearling is a year-old animal, like a horse or a cow.

⊢Cobra⊣

What is a cobra? A cobra is a snake that has a hood. It is poisonous.

⊢Viper⊣

What is a viper? A viper is a poisonous snake. There are two kinds native to Israel—the horned viper and the sawscale, or carpet viper.

BIBLE ANIMAL FACTS
⊢ALL ANIMALS LIVE TOGETHER PEACEFULLY⊣
(ISAIAH 11:6–9; REVELATION 20:1–6, 12)

This story takes up where the last one stopped. Jesus and His armies have come from heaven. Jesus has defeated His enemies who rebelled against Him. John goes on to tell what he sees next in his vision:

"I saw an angel coming down from heaven with a key to the Abyss (also called the bottomless pit). The angel had a great chain. He seized that old snake, Satan, and bound him with the chain. He put him in the Abyss to stay there for 1,000 years. He locked up the Abyss and sealed it."

With Satan in the bottomless pit, what happens on earth for a thousand years? Jesus will reign over the earth, and believers will reign with Him. It will be a time of great peace. All things will be fair and right. King Jesus will not allow any sin to ruin things. All nature will be as it was when God first created the earth.

The wolf will live with the lamb, the leopard will lie down with the goat; and the calf, the lion, and the yearling will be together. No animal will be hurt. A child will lead these animals and will be safe. The cow and bear will feed beside each other, and their babies will lie down together. A baby will play near the hole of the cobra, and the young child will put his hand into the viper's nest. The lion will eat straw like the ox.

When the thousand years are over, Satan will be released from the Abyss. He will gather people from all over the world to battle against King Jesus and the believers. They will surround the camp of God's people, but fire will come down from heaven and devour them. Then Satan will be thrown into the lake of burning sulfur, where he will be tormented day and night forever.

King Jesus will sit on a great white throne, and all the dead unbelievers will be made alive. All unbelievers will stand before Jesus to be judged. The book of life will be opened. It contains the names of all believers. The unbelievers' names won't be there, and they will all be thrown into the lake of fire.

Then there will be a new heaven and a new earth, for the first heaven and earth will pass away in a fire. The Holy City, called the New Jerusalem, will come down out of heaven. God and all believers will live there. There will be no more tears or troubles, no sickness or death. There will be no more darkness, for Jesus is the Light.

A fantastic time is coming! It will begin when Jesus comes in the air to take believers to heaven. Jesus says to everyone, "Behold, I am coming soon! My reward is with Me, and I will give to everyone according to what he has done."

⊢HOW THIS ANIMAL TALE CAN HELP YOU⊣

Will you be in heaven someday? It depends on whether or not your name is in the book of life. How can you know if it is? The moment you believe in Jesus as your Savior, God writes your name there. If it is, you won't be at the great white throne judgment. You will already be enjoying heaven and God's wonderful blessings. If you have not believed in Jesus, would you like to do so now? *(See the last page of this book.)*

⊢BIBLE ANIMAL TALES
REVIEW⊣

Use the clues below to identify the animals' names that go in the puzzle.

ACROSS

  1. I am a great ___; I swallowed Jonah.

  5. I am the largest kind of bird.

  8. I talked to Balaam.

10. God kept us from eating Daniel.

11. We ate up all the plants in Egypt.

13. Absalom rode me and hung in a tree.

16. A shepherd boy killed a lion and me.

DOWN

  1. We hopped all over Pharaoh's palace.

  2. I am a large pig—one "tabooed" animal Peter saw.

  3. Jesus sent demons into us.

  4. We heard an angel talk about a Baby.

  6. I talked to Eve.

  7. We ate Queen Jezebel.

  9. Noah sent me from the ark 3 times.

12. We brought a bride to Isaac.

14. Abel offered me on his altar.

15. Abraham offered me, not Isaac.

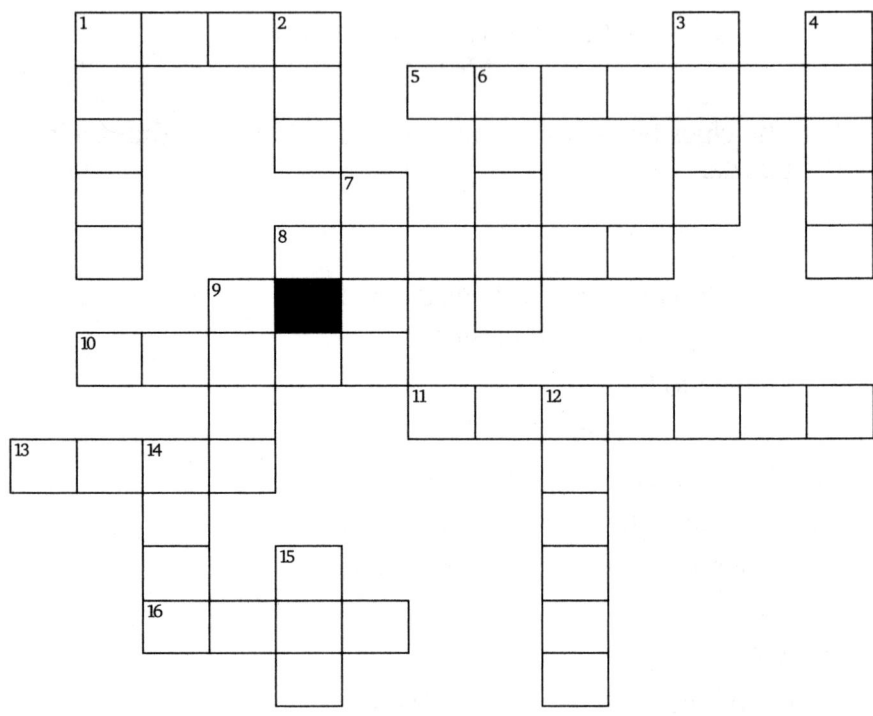

Answers
to the
Puzzles

DEVOTION 1
The Son of God.
Jesus.

DEVOTION 2

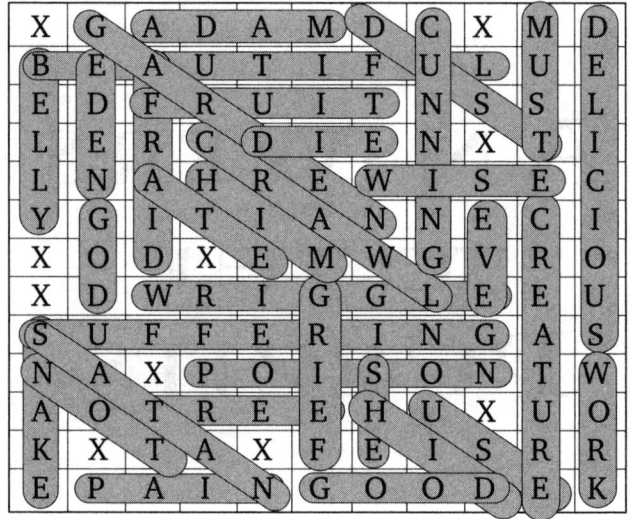

DEVOTION 3
"He was led like a lamb to the slaughter."

DEVOTION 4

1-CAMEL	2-HORSE	3-SHEEP	4-SNAKE
5-GOAT	6-MULE	7-DOVE	8-LAMB
9-DONKEY	10-PIG	11-LION	12-DOG

CREATED BY GOD

DEVOTION 5
earth, wicked, Noah, send, floodwaters, destroy, all, life.
"Never again will the waters become a flood to destroy all life."

DEVOTION 6
1-H, 2-C, 3-G, 4-A, 5-J, 6-D, 7-I, 8-F, 9-B, 10-E

DEVOTION 7
Across: 2-well, 3-robe, 6-boat, 8-angel, 9-manger, 10-cross
Down: 1-tomb, 4-sheep, 5-star

DEVOTION 8
PRAYING, DAILY, HEART, GIVEN, FAITH, BELIEVE
OUR HEAVENLY FATHER

DEVOTION 9
Seek first God's kingdom and his righteousness. Then God will give us all these things.

DEVOTION 10
1-FAITHFUL   2-OBEY GOD   3-NO

DEVOTION 11
Ways of God: Prayer to God, Bible, Godly Parents, Christian Church.
Ways of Satan: Ouija Board, Witchcraft, Fortune Telling, Horoscope.

DEVOTION 12
God: 1-lives forever; 2-knows everything; 3-sees all things; 4-can do anything He wants to do; 5-is love; 6-never changes; 7-is always fair and right.

DEVOTION 13
1—appearance, heart, secrets, deceitful, believe, confess, saved.
2—Jesus, love all, heart, all, soul, all, mind, treasure, heaven, heart.

DEVOTION 14
Our sins.

DEVOTION 15
1-D, 2-F, 3-A, 4-C, 5-G, 6-E, 7-H, 8-B

DEVOTION 16
"Trust in the Lord with all your heart and lean not on your own understanding."

DEVOTION 17
1-parents, 2-health, 3-rainfall, 4-friends,5-kinfolks, 6- food, 7-house, 8-Bible, 9-sunshine, 10-eyes, 11-ears, 12-clothes

DEVOTION 18
Jesus.

DEVOTION 19

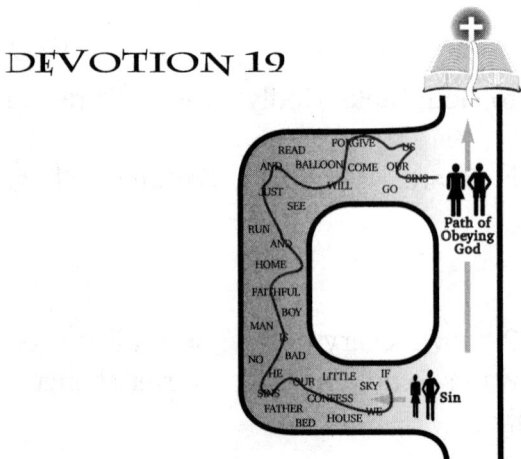

DEVOTION 20
"Some trust in chariots and some in horses, but we trust in the name of the Lord our God."

DEVOTION 21
(The answers are found in the verses given.)

DEVOTION 22
Read the Bible and pray early in the day.

DEVOTION 23
OFFERINGS, BURNT, OBEYING, LORD, VOICE, DELIGHT, AND, SACRIFICES, DOES.
"To obey is better than sacrifice."

DEVOTION 24
"Do not fear, for I am with you; do not be dismayed, for I am your God. I will strengthen you and help you; I will uphold you with my righteous right hand."

DEVOTION 25
(Sinner) 1-sinned. 2-died. 3-turn, sins. 4-believe.
(Christian) 1-sorry. 2-confess. 3-not to sin. 4-people, things, places.

DEVOTION 26
Across: 1-David; 5-forest; 6-revolt; 7-mule; 8-horses; 9-chariot; 11-handsome; 12-Jordan.
Down: 2-Absalom; 3-defeated; 4-killed; 7-messages; 10-hair.

DEVOTION 27
Eagle, nest, hovers, young, wings, catch, carries, pinions.

DEVOTION 28

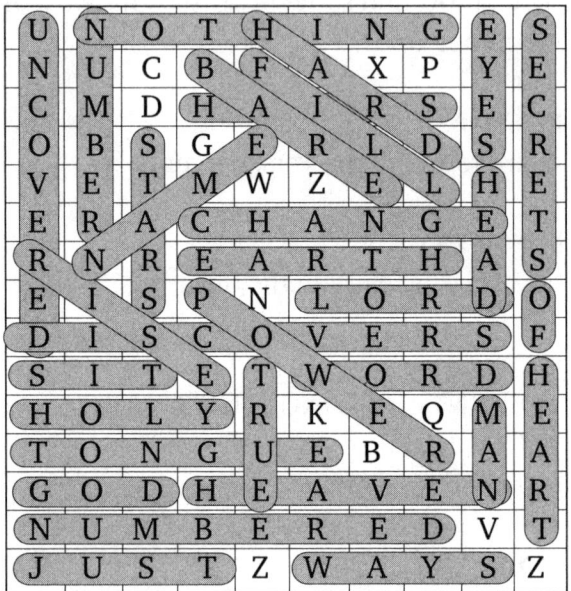

DEVOTION 29
"Whom shall I send? And who will go for us?"
"Here am I. Send me."

DEVOTION 30
walked, chariot, horses, fire, heaven, whirlwind, cloak, river, struck, parted, dry, God, miracles.

DEVOTION 31
"Be praise and honor and glory and power for ever and ever!"

DEVOTION 32
"The wages of sin is death."
"The gift of God is eternal life in Christ Jesus our Lord."

DEVOTION 33
Town, Joppa, ship, deck, water, fish, land, Nineveh. A "V" for victory.

DEVOTION 34
enter, city, shoot, arrow, come, shield, build, siege, ramp, way, came, return, enter, city, defend, city, save.
Yes.

DEVOTION 35
"If anyone would come after me, he must deny himself and take up his cross and follow me."

DEVOTION 36
(The answer is in 1 Peter 5:5,6.)

DEVOTION 37
Jesus was born in Bethlehem—Micah 5:2; Matthew 2:6.
Jesus arose from the dead—Psalm 49:15; Matthew 28:6,7.
Nails pierced Jesus' hands and feet—Psalm 22:16; John 19:37.
Immanuel (Jesus) was born to the Virgin Mary—Isaiah 7:14; Matthew 1:23.
Judas betrayed Jesus—Psalm 41:9; John 13:18, 26.

DEVOTION 38
clear, dear; love, above; Lord, Word; say, Day.

DEVOTION 39
world, everyone; family, friends, neighbors, teachers, schoolmates.

DEVOTION 40

The Bible is all true, for God wrote it. It tells me how to be saved and how to live right. I love it and will try to obey it.

DEVOTION 41

Answered: mean, thank, praise, answer, time, forgive, needs, God.

Prayers: people, pray, alone, day, snake, scorpion, fish.

DEVOTION 42

Peter, Andrew, James, John, Philip, Bartholomew, Thomas, Matthew, James, Thaddeus, Simon, Judas.

DEVOTION 43

Praise the Lord.

DEVOTION 44

Worship in spirit and in truth.

DEVOTION 45

1-L, 2-D, 3-D, 4-L, 5-L, 6-D, 7-L, 8-L, 9-D, 10-D, 11-L, 12-L

DEVOTION 46

The Lamb of God.

DEVOTION 47

I love you. I give my life to you. I will be what you want me to be.

DEVOTION 48

races, world, friends, family, strangers, neighbors, schoolmates, enemies.

DEVOTION 49

DEVOTION 50

Across: 1-fish; 5-ostrich; 8-donkey; 10-lions; 11-locusts; 13-mule; 16-bear.

Down: 1-frogs; 2-hog; 3-pigs; 4-sheep; 6-snake; 7-dogs; 9-dove; 12-camels; 14-lamb; 15-ram.

Eagle, nest, hovers, young, wings, catch, carries, pinions.

GOD'S WONDERFUL PLAN OF SALVATION

Do you want to receive Jesus as your Savior and Lord? Here's how:

Admit that you have sinned. Sin is doing what God does not want you to do or failing to do what He does want you to do. God is holy, and your sin separates you from Him. All persons were born with a nature that wants to sin, and all have sinned. "For all have sinned and fall short of the glory of God" (Romans 3:23).

Repent of your sin. To repent means to be sorry for your sins and turn to God from them. "Repent, then, and turn to God so that your sins may be wiped out" (Acts 3:19).

Know that Jesus, God's Son, died on the cross for your sins and rose again. Jesus never sinned, so He could be punished for us. "Christ died for our sins according to the Scriptures, . . . he was buried, . . . he was raised on the third day. . . " (1 Corinthians 15:3,4).

Believe in Jesus as your Savior and Lord. "Believe in the Lord Jesus Christ, and you will be saved" (Acts 16:31). "To all who received him, to those who believed in his name, he gave the right to become children of God" (John 1:12).

To receive Jesus, you may pray something like this, if you really mean it:

> *Dear Jesus, I know I have sinned. I am sorry for my sins, and I want to turn away from them. I believe You died on the cross for my sins and rose again. Please come into my heart and wash away my sins with Your blood. Amen.*

Thank God for saving you. "Whoever believes in the Son has eternal life" (John 3:36).